Kings and Commoners

1901–1936

The Coronation Durbar at Delhi, 1911. George V and Queen Mary receive the homage of the Indian people on the first-ever visit of a British Sovereign to the Indian sub-continent.

RICHARD POULTON

Head of History, Bryanston School

Kings and Commoners

1901–1936

WORLD'S WORK LTD

To acknowledge accurately the help given in the writing of this book is impossible, for many colleagues, friends and pupils have offered ideas, opinions and encouragement at crucial moments. I am most grateful to them all even though they remain largely anonymous.

Some names must be picked out. Pauline Benefield was primarily responsible for finding the majority of the illustrations in the Radio Times Hulton Picture Library. Sheila Lowe most generously translated the manuscript into legible typescript, helped by Robina Wandel. I am most grateful to Eric Rennick who drew the maps. My thanks go also to David Elliot, Robert Aspinall, and the staff of World's Work for all aspects of their help.

One name stands literally and metaphorically above the rest. The dedication of this book to my wife Sally is only a meagre token of love and gratitude.

First published by
World's Work Ltd
The Windmill Press, Kingswood, Tadworth, Surrey

Filmset and printed in Great Britain by
BAS Printers Limited, Over Wallop, Hampshire

SBN 437 67661 7

To Sally

Contents

CHAPTER ONE

The Kings   1901–1914

"The King lives."

The statement of fact was also a royal command. The new monarch watched with sharp eyes as a sailor moved smartly forward to raise the Royal Standard from half-mast. Though Queen Victoria's body lay in its little coffin on the deck of the Royal Yacht *Alberta*, Edward VII did not intend to be dominated by his mother any longer. As the *Victoria and Albert* followed the *Alberta* through the two lines of warships that stretched from the Isle of Wight to Portsmouth, the flag at the masthead saluted the living king, while the guns of the warships boomed out their final solemn salute to the dead queen. It was January 1901; Edward was nearly sixty years old, and he had been waiting for his inheritance for a long time.

The oak box which was so tenderly transported from Osborne House on the Isle of Wight to the Mausoleum at Frogmore near Windsor contained more than the mortal remains of Victoria; in a way, it also held the remains of an era, which had been Victoria's because of the length of her reign, the dignity of her person and the increasing affection and admiration of her subjects. Men and women knelt in the fields as her funeral train passed on its way from the South Coast to Victoria Station in London. As her coffin was taken across to Paddington on a gun-carriage, the city took on the quiet of a church. The streets were hung with purple and white draperies, for Victoria had forbidden the use of black, and each silent bystander was acutely aware of the end of a remarkable reign, and the beginning of a strange new age. For a short time, London stopped, to pay its last respects.

At Windsor, the calm, sad reverence was interrupted briefly. One of the Royal Artillery horses harnessed to the gun-carriage on which the coffin was to travel to the castle became restless, and finally it reared up and broke its traces. The remaining horses, clearly unsettled, were quickly unhitched and led away, and into their place came a detachment of sailors who had been drawn up on guard near the station. The tough communication cords of nearby railway carriages were fashioned into makeshift tow

Ships and sailors make
ready for the Royal Yacht
Alberta as it brings
Victoria's body to the
mainland.

ropes, and with these and the animal harnesses, men rather than
beasts drew the body of the dead queen along the processional
route to St George's Chapel. It was the only change in the broad
outline of the funeral arrangements that Victoria herself had
made three years before.

But change was what people expected now. The Victorian Age
belonged to the nineteenth century, and it had grown old and
prim as the Queen had aged. Not only the horse was going to kick
over the traces. Beneath the surface of English life there was
restless energy and new vigour which was waiting to challenge
the old ideas and values. Edward's ways were not going to be the
same as his mother's, a fact which she had always known and
always feared. Her constant worries about Edward were not
shared by the whole country, though *The Times* did write in 1901
"There is no position in the world more difficult to fill than that
of Heir-Apparent to the throne . . . It must be with a feeling akin
to hopelessness that a man in that position offers up the familiar
prayer 'Lead us not into temptation'." But to many people,
Edward was a man of fashion, an up-to-date and attractive figure,
a welcome change after the stuffy atmosphere of the Court in the
past few years.

There had been plenty of new inventions and advances in
Victoria's reign, yet while the old lady was alive, the old patterns

Bluejackets dragging the funeral gun-carriage through the crowded streets of Windsor. Edward VII follows, with Kaiser Wilhelm II of Germany just behind him.

of behaviour were maintained. Now, as he said, "The *King* lives"; it was a signal for a new world, a new century. He knew that people wanted to look forward, not back. The standard of living was rising as the ingenuity of the Victorian inventors was reflected in new machines for homes, offices and factories. Poverty was diminishing in most areas, and life was becoming more adventurous and happier. No longer were the majority of ordinary men working desperately just in order to survive; times were still fairly hard, but there was a feeling of continual improvement, of progress, of change for the better.

Edward was no saint, as everybody knew. They knew that he loved the company of beautiful women; they knew that he owned a number of outstandingly good race-horses which for instance won for him the Grand National, the Derby, the St Leger, and several other major races in one year. He smoked cigarettes, a thing which a public figure was expected not to do, and worse still, his friends knew that he even smoked cigars immediately after dinner. He enjoyed his dinners; they seldom consisted of less than twelve courses, usually of rich flavour and rare quality. Caviare, snipe, truffles, partridge, oysters, quails, nothing was too grand, too expensive, too difficult to obtain for his table.

He enjoyed sailing too, at least while his racing yacht *Britannia* was successful, but after his nephew Kaiser Wilhelm II of

3

Edward was still Prince of Wales when this photograph was taken in 1899. The car, a twelve horse-power Daimler, was capable of 40 m.p.h.

Germany had had two rival yachts built, the second of which was faster than *Britannia*, his enthusiasm waned.

Edward was a more public person than Victoria had been; he was very much a man first and a member of the Royal Family second. He dined in lavish hotels and grand cafes, and spent weekends at the homes of his friends. Twice he appeared in courts of law, as a witness in cases involving divorce or cheating at cards, and it was considered somewhat scandalous that he should have any contact with people who were involved in that sort of behaviour. There seemed to be no end to his novel and daring activities, and so wherever he went and whatever he did, he was "news", a subject of tittle-tattle and rumour and exaggerated responses. Some people were horrified even when he bought a car for himself.

But despite the people whom he shocked, despite his apparently unsuitable character, Edward brought to the throne of England the human element which it needed in 1901. When Victoria had succeeded in 1837, the monarchy was despised by many. "His late Majesty," wrote *The Spectator* when William IV died in that year, "though at times a jovial and, for a king, an honest man, was a weak, ignorant, commonplace sort of person . . . His very popularity was acquired at the price of something like public contempt." Victoria's reign, and the fact that she had

Edward VII shooting at Sandringham with his friends. c. 1907.

been very withdrawn for much of it, had changed the image of the monarchy. It was considered by some to be almost mystical, a thing to be worshipped and reverenced and admired from afar. Most monarchies in Europe were treated similarly, and most monarchies in Europe were going to disappear in the course of the next generation or so. Edward made the British monarchy more acceptable to his people, and gave it a cheerful, practical, lively image which was to carry it through many political troubles in the twentieth century. His faults were also his attractive qualities. His personality dominated Court circles and yet also was such that he was constantly referred to in the new popular newspapers. The nine years of his reign were an essential part of English development in matters of politics and foreign affairs and even of the whole constitution. To the surprise of many, Edward played an important part in all of these.

So too did his son George V, though in a very different style. Whereas his father had delighted in the cries of "Good old Teddie!" which had greeted him from time to time, George was a quieter, more reserved person who would have been embarrassed by such behaviour. He was a naval officer by training, a strict and respectable family man by instinct, and a calm, methodical monarch by choice. His private hobbies were stamp collecting, shooting and yachting, and he had no desire for the

George V riding in London.

glamour and publicity of his father's way of life. He had dignity, courage and wisdom, and these virtues were needed frequently in his reign of twenty-five and a half years. Edward's reign had shown that the monarchy was still an effective and lively part of the British constitution; it was George who had to prove what this meant in practice. The decisions which he took affected every aspect of life in a tense quarter-century. He inherited "the Edwardian age" and for four years there was little obvious change, but thereafter he guided the country through war against Germany, civil disorder in England and Ireland, economic distress and misery and social and political upheaval. To the very end, he served his people. On the day of his death, when he was so ill that he could scarcely write his initials on a document that he had to sign for the Privy Council, he refused to allow anyone to guide his hand, but summoned up enough strength to apologise to his Councillors around his bed: "Gentlemen, I am sorry for keeping you waiting like this—I am unable to concentrate." It was as close to an admission of defeat as he had ever made, but he signed the paper. Like Edward VII, George V knew what had to be done, and in their own ways, they each did it.

CHAPTER TWO

The Commoners 1901–1914

Edward VII was crowned in August 1902, nineteen months after his accession. The Coronation was delayed by the long-drawn out negotiations to bring the Boer War to an end, and further because the King was struck down by appendicitis just three days before the date originally chosen. At that time the operation was still regarded as serious and potentially very dangerous, and the tension of the occasion forged a strong emotional link between Edward and his subjects, and made the Coronation when it did occur a day of outstanding relief and celebration. The best expression of pride and joy that remains unchanged since 1902 is the final section of the music of the "Commemorative Ode for the Coronation of King Edward VII", written by Dr Edward Elgar.

The Coronation portrait; Edward VII and his Queen, Alexandra.

Sir Edward Elgar, photographed in 1924 while conducting 'Land of Hope and Glory' at the opening of the British Empire Exhibition.

Better known as the *Pomp and Circumstance March No. 1,* it was in fact a tune which he had composed previously and which had already been published. After receiving from Elgar some nonsense words to indicate the rhythm of the music, a master at Eton wrote the verse which captured the spirit of the whole nation at the time of the Coronation:

"Land of Hope and Glory, Mother of the free,
How shall we extol thee, who are born of thee?
Wider still and wider shall thy bounds be set;
God, who made thee mighty, make thee mightier yet . . ."

When the Coronation Ode was first performed in Queen's Hall, London, in 1902, Elgar was called back to the conductor's rostrum five times to acknowledge the frantic applause.

Hope and glory, might and freedom, and wide, wide bounds: these were the things that Britons thought they saw in Britain and her Empire in Edward's reign. They were not mistaken. In the Fiji Islands, the last link was completed in an all-British submarine telegraph cable which circled the earth and linked all the colonies and dominions directly with England. Captain Robert Scott, probing further south than any man had done before, discovered new land on the Antarctic continent which he immediately named King Edward VII Land. In east Africa, British engineers were building the six hundred miles of the Uganda Railway, from Lake Victoria Nyanza to the sea at Mombasa; the train that ran on this improbable line got the affectionate nickname of the "Lunatic Express", and symbolized the crazy confidence of the age and of the British people. 1902 was also the year in which Cecil Rhodes, the greatest of the Imperial architects, died in South Africa, leaving in his will instructions that "Rhodes Scholarships" should be created out of his vast wealth, by which students from all over the world could come to Oxford University, there to learn all the advantages of cultured British society. As far as most educated Englishmen were concerned, Britannia still ruled the waves and many of the lands beyond the waves, if not directly, then at least by virtue of a general

Robert Scott's ship *Discovery* in the Antarctic, 1902. The hydrogen balloon used for observation is being deflated after its first ascent. On the rigging of *Discovery* hangs part of the ship's provisions—frozen seal meat.

civilising influence which was uniquely and somehow unsurprisingly British. The words of the Coronation Ode were not inappropriate, though it would be misleading to claim that they gave the whole picture.

Life was indeed exciting and proud and adventurous, provided that you were a member of the right social grouping. In 1904, the Motor Car Act came into force. Those who were rich enough to own a car (and there were then over eight thousand cars in Britain) were allowed to travel at speeds up to twenty miles an hour, as long as the car and the driver were fully registered. Those who had large estates enjoyed their shooting: King Edward and six friends killed 3,937 pheasants in one day. Court circles included many true aristocrats with their homes in the country and in London, whose way of life was always calm and genteel; they had many duties to perform which they carried out with conscientious care, but they were a small and privileged group who enjoyed the fruits of power and responsibility without the restrictions of the Victorian age. The Prime Minister in 1902 was Lord Salisbury; his nephew Arthur Balfour was Leader of the House of Commons; another nephew and a cousin were members of the Cabinet, and a son and another more distant relative were in junior ministerial posts. The government of the

9

High fashion at Henley Regatta, 1914.

country did not require the constant presence of the Prime Minister, however, and for much of the year Lord Salisbury was in the habit of spending his time at one of his houses, not in England but in France. Those who traditionally were the leaders of society were still in their place, as yet unchallenged by the stirrings below the surface.

They were well supported by the upper middle classes, whose comfort also was a matter of great importance and concern, at least to themselves and to those whom they employed for the purpose. There was no scarcity of well-trained servants for the house, nor for the gardens and grounds, nor for transport, whichever type of "horse-power" was involved. Indeed, there was more division amongst the different types of servant than there was amongst their employers. Butler, coachman (or chauffeur), cook, housekeeper, gamekeeper: these were the "aristocrats" among the throng below stairs, whose words were law to the housemaids, kitchen maids, grooms and gardeners, and whose pride in their position of service was one reason why the system lasted so long. It was not high pay which earned their loyalty, for a domestic servant in London at the turn of the century earned about £18 a year (less elsewhere), and a girl under the age of sixteen got about £8 a year as her wages, together with her keep and her uniform. Even a highly trained and respectable butler could be employed for not much more than £60 a year. Perhaps it was a sense of belonging, a sense of being needed, which kept these servants so devoted to "their" families; nanny or nursemaid, parlour-maid or stable-lad, they knew their place, and were content in its security, despite the bells that were rung for them, the restrictions that were put on them and the hours and hours of service that were expected of them. "Ladies were ladies in those days; they did not do things themselves, they told other people what to do and how to do it" wrote Gwen Raverat in her book of recollections called *Period Piece*. She shows how the upper middle class family was waited on hand and foot: "Aunt Etty . . . told me, when she was eighty-six, that she had never made a pot of tea in her life; and that she had never in all her days been out in the dark alone, not even in a cab; and I don't believe she had ever travelled by train without a maid . . . Once she wrote when her maid, the patient and faithful Janet, was away for a day or two: 'I am very busy answering my own bell'."

Open-topped motor coaches challenge the horse-drawn cabs.
Piccadilly Circus in 1912.

11

An elaborate
day dress, 1905.

With this class of people came new pastimes and pursuits; croquet on the lawn, music and amateur theatricals in the drawing room; luncheon parties in the winter and garden parties in the summer; fashionable holidays abroad or at one or two carefully selected places in England. It was a life secure in its setting, familiar, friendly and free from artificial restraint. All it depended on was a magical mixture of at least two of the following ingredients: money, parentage, talent and luck. The population of Edwardian Britain passed through the 40,000,000 mark. Of these, 39,000,000 earned less than £3 a week; only 10,000 earned more than £13 a week. The traditional aristocrats and the upper middle classes were the tiny tip of a very broad-based pyramid, and it was in the reign of Edward VII that social changes (which Victoria's reign had both made possible and yet postponed) began to shift the base of the pyramid and thus crack the apparently solid structure of English society. In the nine years that Edward was on the throne, the whole emphasis of English politics changed in such a way that English society could never be the same again.

It was not that the poorer classes were being deliberately oppressed by the traditionally rich and powerful. On the contrary, there were better prospects for most people as more and more men got the vote, and more and more children went to school. The vote had been extended by Reform Acts in 1867 and 1884, so that nearly seven million males over the age of twenty-one had the right to elect the Government, and education had been extended since Forster's Act of 1870 by several other acts, and then remodelled by the Education Act of 1902, which gave county and county borough councils responsibility not only for primary education but also for all forms of secondary school. It was because members of the working sections of the population were able to play an informed and intelligent part in the democratic process that the "golden summer" of Edwardian England became stormy and unsettled.

With the exception of the years 1892–1895, when the Liberals were in power but able to achieve very little, the Conservative party governed England from 1886 until 1905. Both parties were largely aristocratic; even the Liberals in 1894 had Prime Minister, Foreign Secretary and four other members of the Cabinet in the House of Lords. Both parties believed that they were able to represent the views of the working classes and take full account of what the workers needed; both parties failed to convince the workers. The Liberal party tried to include among its Members of

Primary Education for all; a nature study class in 1908.

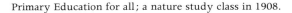

Parliament men who could speak with authority for the poorer classes, men like John Burns who had left school at the age of 10 to work in a Battersea candle factory. He became an engineer and a good political speaker, and in 1892 he was elected M.P. for Battersea. But Burns and other similar men needed their own party, and in 1900 the Labour Representation Committee was formed, to be remodelled in 1906 under the name of the "Labour Party". Parliament had to adapt itself to the needs of this new group. Not only did they express new ideas; not only did they have a "cloth cap" image instead of the standard top hat ideal; they were also neither able nor prepared to be amateur politicians. The early representatives came from mining or shipbuilding or industrial work in the Midlands; they had given up their jobs in order to proclaim the Labour message, and so they needed to be paid as Members of Parliament. As one of them wrote "It was some weeks before I paid my first visit to the Members' dining-room, as I had been warned by an old member that the prices there were beyond the means of a Labour member. He accordingly put me in the way of obtaining refreshment in a very comfortable tea-room where a meal was beautifully served at the democratic price of one shilling (5p)." In 1910, therefore, special provision was made for all M.P.s to be paid; governing was henceforth not just a right of the rich, but a task to which any man could aspire.

In those early years of the Labour movement, before it became confident of its future, the Conservatives were also divided and uncertain. They had been embarrassed by the Boer War and its aftermath, and were shortly afterwards split from top to bottom by doubts about Free Trade, the system by which countries traded freely with each other without putting tariffs or customs duties on each other's goods. This system had existed throughout the second half of the nineteenth century, when Britain had grown rich and powerful. But it was now suggested by Joseph Chamberlain, a Conservative (or "Unionist" as they were then known—see Chapter 5) Cabinet Minister, that Britain's future

VOTE FOR

Home Rule.

Democratic Government.

Justice to Labour

No Monopoly.

No Landlordism

Temperance Reform.

Healthy Homes.

Fair Rents.

Eight-Hour Day.

Work for the Unemployed.

KEIR HARDIE.

The new image of politics: A poster from 1895.

wealth and power could only be safeguarded by closer links with the Empire. He proposed that Free Trade should stop, and that tariffs should be placed on most imports, while the British Empire should come together like some huge business organisation, protecting and giving preference to its own members. From the middle of 1903 until December 1905, the argument between Imperial Preference and Free Trade swayed backwards and forwards, until the Prime Minister Balfour could no longer hold his Conservative and Unionist party together. He offered his resignation to Edward VII, who approached the Liberals to see whether they could form a government. Under Sir Henry Campbell-Bannerman, they could, and did, and the country confirmed them in power early in 1906 with a huge majority of 354 seats. So began one of the most brilliant ministries of the twentieth century, filled with able men like Asquith, Lloyd George, Churchill, Grey, Haldane—and also including John Burns. The significance of this was that even the Liberal Party with its overwhelming majority was finding it necessary to change its attitudes and its approach in the twentieth century, and all the tensions of post-Victorian change suddenly erupted over two related issues—the People's Budget, and the reform of the House of Lords.

The new Liberal philosophy was that the State should look after its poorer or weaker members. Gladstone, the greatest Liberal Leader of the nineteenth century, had always fought for fairness and equality of opportunity, but had usually avoided the spending of much government money. The twentieth-century Liberals became intent upon being like Robin Hood, getting money from the rich to pay for the better welfare of the poor. So

15

Slum children outside a London East End shop, 1910.

they passed an Act in 1906 which allowed free meals for needy children at school, and in 1908 they made an Old Age Pensions Act, which entitled anyone over 70 who had an income of less than ten shillings (50p) a week to receive a further 5/- (25p) from the State. This was a small beginning, costing the Government only just over £1 million a year, but it was enough to raise the expectations of the poor and the fears and fury of the rich, especially when even the method of paying for these reforms became in itself a method of reform. Faced with a need for an extra £16,000,000 in his Budget in 1909 to pay for social reforms and for the new Dreadnought battleships (see Chapter 4), the Chancellor of the Exchequer, David Lloyd George, decided to institute a number of new and challenging taxes. A tax on petrol and on motor licences hit the rich, as did an increase in income tax and a new "super-tax" on incomes of more than £3,000 a year, though on the other hand people with children under the age of 16 were allowed to pay slightly less income tax. There was also a 20% tax on any increase in the value of land when it changed hands, as well as an increase in the tax paid on tobacco and spirits. The effect was to demand more from the rich, which was why the budget was soon referred to as "The People's Budget".

But it was not so much the money that was at stake; it was the whole principle of government. The Conservatives in the House of Lords in 1909 decided that the time had come to challenge the novel approach of the Liberals. Lloyd George carried the fight back to them; the House of Lords, he declared, was not so much "the watchdog of the Constitution but Mr Balfour's poodle". The sense of humour of their Lordships did not stretch far enough to take this and other verbal insults. Less than four weeks after the Commons had passed the Budget by 379 votes to 149, the Lords rejected it by 350 votes to 75. The Liberal Government could not govern without the money which the Budget would have provided, and did not wish to govern while the Lords felt so free to reject many Liberal policies. Not only the Budget had been destroyed; in earlier years Education Bills had been vetoed, as had a Licencing Bill which was intended to cut down the terrible social evil of drunkenness, and, in the more distant past, Gladstone's final effort to solve the Irish problem by granting Home Rule to the Irish. There had to be a showdown now.

Asquith, the Liberal Prime Minister since 1908, asked Edward to dissolve Parliament, and in January 1910 a new election was held. The Liberals won 275 seats in the Commons; the Conservative and Unionist party won 273. But the battle was not as close as these figures might make it seem. Also elected were 40 members of the Labour party and 82 Irish Nationalists, and these two groups had their own obvious reasons for supporting the Liberals, and opposing the House of Lords. After Asquith had announced the ways in which he intended the powers of the House of Lords to be restricted, and after these had been approved in principle by the Commons, the People's Budget was re-introduced. It passed the Commons with a majority of 92 on April 27th 1910, and on the next day the Lords passed it on to the King for approval without voting on it again. They had lost the financial half of the battle and they knew it. What no-one knew was that eight days later, Edward VII would be dead, of bronchitis and heart trouble. His final words were "No, I shall not give in; I shall go on; I shall work to the last."

17

H. H. Asquith,
Prime Minister
of the reforming
Liberal Ministry
from 1908 to 1916.

The public were stunned by the news. It was less than a year since Edward's horse Minoru had won the Derby and caused one of the greatest spontaneous displays of enthusiasm for royalty that the country had seen. Thousands of race-goers sang *God Save the King,* and even the policemen on duty waved their helmets in the air as the crowd cheered. A year after Edward's death, as the battle over the powers of the House of Lords struggled to its conclusion, Conservatives in the House of Commons screamed at Asquith "Who killed the King?", as if blaming the Liberal ministry for putting unnecessary strain on Edward over the People's Budget.

The voters did not blame the Liberals. After Edward's son, George V, had come to the throne, and after he had most reluctantly given a secret promise that he would create sufficient Liberal peers to enforce changes in the House of Lords if Asquith were to win another General Election, Parliament was dissolved again. In December, the second General Election of 1910 was held. The Liberals won the same number of seats as the Conservatives and Unionists (272), and so once again the Irish Nationalists (84) and the Labour Party (42) held the future in their hands. They still supported the Liberals for their own individual reasons, and they ensured that the "Parliament Bill" restricting the powers of the House of Lords passed the Commons in May 1911. The Bill proposed, as Asquith had suggested in 1910, that the House of Lords could have no power over money bills at all, and that over other public bills, they only had power to reject them in two successive sessions. If the Commons were to pass a bill in three successive sessions despite rejection by the Lords, that bill could then go to the monarch for approval, and could become an Act. Thus the Lords would never again have a complete veto, except in one specific instance, which was if the Commons were to try to pass a bill changing the length of Parliaments. The maximum length was fixed at five years.

Obviously the Lords had no wish to give in to these reforms, which were bound to weaken the considerable hold that they had over matters in Parliament. But many lords recognised that the spirit of Edwardian, and now Georgian, England required a new spirit of government. In the end, in August 1911, the Parliament Bill was passed in the Lords by 131 votes to 114, with many members abstaining rather than casting their vote against what they viewed as regrettable but inevitable change. It was just over ten years since Victoria had died, and already the political and social situation of the country was greatly altered.

Outwardly, the age was still "Edwardian", and despite the change of monarch, that adjective is normally used to cover the years up to 1914. Politics were changing, but the politicians were the same men as before. Their wives wore the same kinds of clothes, and they all went to the same social functions. Ascot, Henley and Cowes were still the places for the rich, fashionable and leisured people to be seen, though there was a new art form to patronise also, for in 1911 Diaghilev brought his company of Russian dancers to London. Society ladies flocked to see Anna Pavlova, Tamara Karsavina and Nijinsky in the most exciting and accomplished ballet that had ever been seen on the English stage. Unlike in Paris, where the first performance of Stravinsky's *Rite of Spring* ended in a riot, in London the dance and the dancers were ecstatically received—after the music critic of the *Daily*

19

Telegraph had come on stage to explain the strange new sounds of the music.

For those who preferred, or could only afford, simpler pleasures at the theatre, the Edwardian Music Hall went on with its "naughty but nice" songs and dances and comedians, though by 1914 there were signs of new things coming, in the shape of occasional snatches of "ragtime" music, or, at the end of a live performance, a few frames of flickering film. Neither was yet attracting serious consideration; at this level, neither the music nor the mood had changed with the monarch. Perhaps there was a vague sense that change was coming; women were arguing for the right to vote; Ireland was a restless land, uncertain of its future; workers were banding together more strongly, demanding better conditions and new business organisations. But the Edwardian age still lingered on into the hot summer of 1914. The changes that the autumn would bring were beyond imagination.

CHAPTER THREE

War and the Western Front 1914–1918

The young man Gavrilo Princip from Serbia walked away from the main avenue of Sarajevo, out of the sunshine and into the welcome shade of Franz Josef Street. Clearly the attempt to assassinate the Archduke Franz Ferdinand of Austria had failed, and he needed time to think out what should be his next move. The plan had been for a number of assassins to wait along the processional route of the heir to the Austrian throne; one or other of them must surely be successful, but something had gone totally wrong. What Princip did not know was that the first would-be assassin had lost his nerve completely; the second had thrown a bomb at the Archduke's open car, but the Archduke had deflected it down into the road while his driver, sensing trouble, had accelerated. The bomb hit the ground and exploded just in front of the next car in the procession, injuring a senior official.

With great courage and calm, Franz Ferdinand and his wife

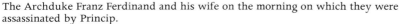

The Archduke Franz Ferdinand and his wife on the morning on which they were assassinated by Princip.

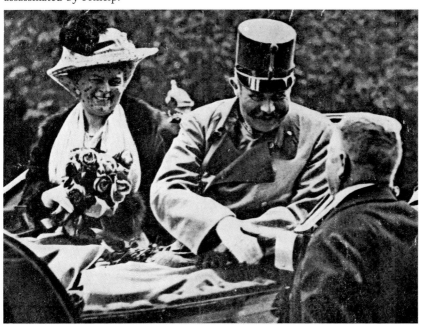

21

continued their official functions, but decided to include a visit to the wounded man in hospital. Unfortunately nobody told the chauffeur about the change of plans, and he drove along the route that had been originally planned until a sharp order from a general in the car made him pull up hurriedly. He was now told of the change, and accordingly began to back the car out of the street he was in, Franz Josef Street, onto the main avenue. As he did so, he passed within two paces of an incredulous Gavrilo Princip. Without having time to think what he was doing, and knowing only that he had come to Sarajevo to kill the Archduke, Princip took out his pistol and at a range of five feet fired two shots. The first hit the Archduke in the neck; the second hit his wife in the stomach. Within fifteen minutes they were both dead.

Within four and a half years, the total number of deaths which stemmed from Princip's action had become too great to count accurately, but is generally thought to be about twelve million. The number of wounded, even more difficult to count, was probably two and a half times as many, or roughly thirty million. Relatively few came from Serbia, Princip's country, or from Bosnia, the little country of which Sarajevo was the capital and which was under the protection of Austria. Over one million dead and three million wounded came from Austria itself, but the awful truth was that the tension of which Gavrilo Princip was a very small part increased with such rapidity and violence that the casualties came from every continent in the world before the shooting stopped. South America was the only large area to be scarcely affected by the war; elsewhere, existing loyalties as in the British Empire or new worries as in the United States of America or sheer opportunism as in the Far East brought peoples of all colours and creeds into battle. It was truly called the Great War, for the world had never witnessed anything so terrible before, and one of the few good effects of it was that men resolved never to unleash such destruction again. The Great War was also known, therefore, as "the war to end all war"—until in 1939 a new and horrific conflict broke out which was soon known as the

Second World War. Thus the Great War had to be renamed the First World War in the history books, the war that had ended nothing except the existence of a calmer, simpler world.

The road from Princip's action to the outbreak of a world war was not simple, however. It contained many twists and turns and false trails, and its foundations had been laid by previous generations. Princip and his conspirators, melodramatically calling their organisation "The Black Hand", believed that by murdering the heir to the Austrian throne on June 28th 1914, they were helping to create a new united Serbia, free from Austrian domination. The Austrians, by sending an ultimatum to the Serbian government, believed that they were putting Serbia in her place and preventing any greater disorders within their provinces. When Serbia refused to accept two of the conditions of the ultimatum, the Austrians declared war on July 26th, despite the fact that their army was not ready and they knew it. But now the ripples in this pool of bluff and counterbluff began to spread out. Russia, although also unready for war, was not prepared to watch Austria bully Serbia into submission, and had already promised support to Serbia. The Russians had even ordered some of their troops to be mobilised on July 20th; this bluff had not worked (since Austria did declare war on Serbia less than a week later), and so although virtually no actual fighting had yet taken place, the Russians now had to go one step further in their attitude, and mobilise fully, which they did on July 31st. The Austrians therefore did the same, on the same day.

But Germany was pledged to support Austria by a treaty made in 1879, although Germany in turn knew that France was pledged to support Russia by a treaty made in 1894. Therefore two messages went out from the German capital, Berlin, on July 31st. Would the Russians, asked one, stop their mobilisation? The Russians were meant to reply within twelve hours, but no answer came back at all. Would the French, asked the other, remain neutral if Russia and Germany went to war, and indeed hand over two fortresses to Germany as indications of their good faith? The

French did reply, but indignantly, and in the negative. On August 1st Germany declared war on Russia, and on August 2nd demanded the right to march through Belgium in order to protect itself from the French (by striking first). On August 3rd the Germans marched into Belgium, and declared war on France, claiming that French aircraft had attacked German territory.

And what of Britain, the Britain that since the battle of Waterloo ninety-nine years before had tried to keep out of European conflicts, and had succeeded except for the brief upset of the Crimean War? Britain had close diplomatic ties with both France and Russia, but she was not committed to go to war on behalf of either of them. The ripples in the pool might not have reached Britain, but for the fact that in 1839, Britain had guaranteed to protect the independence and neutrality of Belgium. On August 4th 1914, Britain demanded that the Germans should get off Belgian soil. The Germans refused, and Britain therefore declared war on Germany at midnight. To the last, no-one knew what was bluff and what was real; the German Chancellor could not believe that Britain would declare war just for "a scrap of paper", as he described the 1839 treaty. Sir Edward Grey, British Foreign Secretary, was more accurate in his understanding of the situation: "The lamps are going out all over Europe," he said. "We shall not see them lit again in our lifetime."

Grey had good reason for his pessimism. Although peace had turned into widespread war in a little under six weeks in the summer of 1914, there had already been warnings, like distant rumbles of thunder before the oncoming storm.

At the end of the nineteenth century, Europe had divided itself into two armed camps, suspicious of each other and anxious to prevent the other from gaining any advantage anywhere in the world. Germany's alliance with Austria-Hungary and with Italy frightened the Russians and the French into each other's arms, and Britain's lack of official commitment did not mean that the country was not involved in the general tension. Wilhelm II of

The cousins at war. *Left to right:* Wilhelm II wears the uniform of the Death's Head Hussars; George V of England is in naval uniform, and Nicholas II of Russia is in Court Dress. They were all grandsons of Queen Victoria.

Germany and Nicholas II of Russia were cousins, and nephews of Edward VII of England, who spent much of his reign involved in personal diplomacy aimed at keeping calm the relationship between the two younger men and their respective countries and allies. But to English eyes, Wilhelm of Germany often appeared aggressive and challenging, and his country's economic and naval growth did nothing to lessen English worries. Not only had Wilhelm given support to the Boers in South Africa; he had also twice worried all nations that had colonies by disputing France's role in Morocco, and furthermore he was planning to build a railway from Berlin to Baghdad, as though to rival Britain's idea of a line from Cairo to Capetown. His interest in Baghdad meant that he was also interested in the Balkans, through which his line had to run, and so the problems of the declining Turkish Empire attracted increased attention, especially from Russia. It was the Balkan wars of 1912 and 1913 that had encouraged Russia to offer support to Serbia.

The German challenge was not only on the land. In 1897 Wilhelm had appointed Admiral von Tirpitz head of the German Navy, with the express task of building up a powerful war fleet. Britain retaliated by launching H.M.S. *Dreadnought* in 1906, the fastest, heaviest, most armoured and most deadly warship ever devised until then; it was believed that she could sink the whole German navy on her own. Obviously matters could not rest there. The Germans immediately planned their (improved) version of the Dreadnought, and Britain increased her building programme,

A drawing of the launching of HMS *Dreadnought*, the first of a new and deadly class of weapon, in February 1906.

after a slight hesitation. "We want eight, and we won't wait" ran the popular slogan. The "People's Budget" had to raise money for Dreadnoughts as well as for National Insurance schemes, and when war was declared in 1914, Britain had twenty-nine capital ships to Germany's seventeen.

Unexpectedly, it was not these ships that were going to fight the most desperate battles in the war, even though they were the fastest amd most sophisticated weapons of destruction that man had so far invented. The war was destined to be a soldiers' war, a gunners' war, a war in which men burrowed like moles in mud of their own making, and drowned on land. It was to be a war which failed to fit in with anyone's predictions, and although it started between Austria and Serbia and ended with countries as far apart as the United States and China, Rumania and Japan all involved, the conflict had its heart in the battle between the armed camps of Europe which took place on the "Western Front", a shifting, slithering line that snaked from the Flanders coast southwards and eastwards to the Swiss frontier. European history has seldom allowed a strong Germany to coincide with a strong France, and the whole German strategy rested on the speedy elimination of her western neighbour.

Germany's plan for the conquest of France had been made

between 1897 and 1905, by her Chief of Staff, Schlieffen, and its strength rested on the fact that it could achieve the capture of Paris and the surrender of France within six weeks. Once that was done, Germany could turn to face Russia, or any other continental power, without the fear that she would be attacked on two fronts. Speed was the essence of success for Schlieffen, and speed meant a free passage through Belgium. "Get there fustest with the mostest", the recipe for success which had been first enunciated by a general in the American Civil War, summed up the German plan. 840,000 men had to be pumped through the single railway junction of Aachen; 11,000 troop trains were moving simultaneously when full mobilisation took place. Like a giant scythe, the German army swept through Belgium in the middle weeks of August, a precise and time-tabled wave of military might.

But the Belgians and French resisted fiercely, and on August 21st, the British Expeditionary Force reached them near Mons, in the centre of the Franco-Belgian border. On August 22nd they had their first skirmish with the Germans, and on the next day they came into full contact with the enemy. The skilled rapid fire of the British forces, "that contemptible little army" as the Kaiser had called them, scattered the German advance, making them think that the British had twenty-eight machine guns per battalion, though the true figure was only two. Though pulled back immediately, on August 26th the B.E.F. held their line again at Le Cateau, now on French territory, despite the loss of 8,000 men. The Germans in every sector found their progress getting slower and slower. French, Belgian and British counter-attacks were destroying the Schlieffen timetable, and the German belief in their own ability to win easily.

Exhaustion was setting in on both sides; men of the B.E.F. averaged only three or four hours sleep in every twenty-four as they retreated, but the Germans were in greater difficulties as their master plan failed them and their supplies came through irregularly at best. At last Moltke, the German Chief of Staff,

27

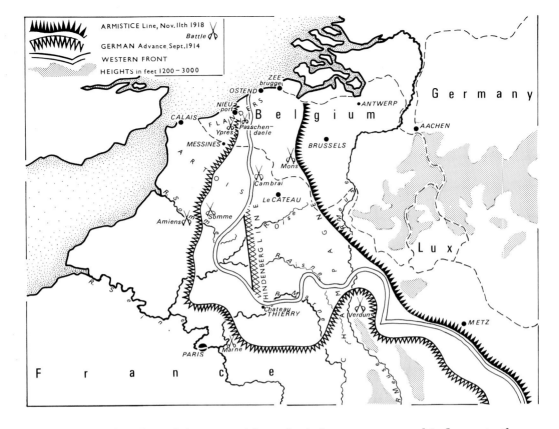

abandoned the timetable and tried to concentrate his forces to the east of Paris. It was a fatal mistake. Though his troops got to within thirty miles of Paris, it was achieved at the cost of a crucial gap between his First and Second Armies. Into this gap came the B.E.F. and the French 5th Army, the latter partly rushed out from Paris in taxicabs, and on September 5th and 6th the German advance was finally stopped and thrust back into retreat. This Battle of the Marne set the tide flowing against Germany for a week, until they dug in on the line of the River Aisne. The British and French were too slow and too tired to prise them out; stalemate started here.

To the west and north of these positions, each commander-in-chief sent troops to try to turn the flank of his enemy; their efforts cancelled each other out as they raced for the sea, but the concentration of troops on both sides brought about one more great spasm of fighting, the first Battle of Ypres. The Kaiser came from Germany hoping to witness his army's triumphal entry into this little town; the battle raged from October 12th to November 11th, with the Germans inching closer and closer to their objective. The Belgians broke dykes at nearby Nieuport, letting in the sea and thus holding that part of the line, but on October 31st, the British section could hold no longer. General Haig led the retreat in order to steady his men. The English General Sir John French sent a message to the French commander, General Foch, asking for assistance and adding that if it did not come, there was "nothing left for me to do but go up and get killed with the British First Corps". Only one battalion, the 2nd Worcestershire Regiment, already reduced to about 350 men, held their ground and then, with inspired leadership and outstanding courage, counter-attacked. The Germans flinched, hesitated, and retreated. The Allied line solidified, and held again. On November 11th, the same situation occurred; this time the brilliant commanding officer of the Worcestershires was killed, but the crack Prussian Guards were repulsed, and the stalemate was complete. From the sea to Switzerland, a new and terrible phenomenon was about to start: trench warfare, in which millions of men were to die while the lines of trenches moved not

British troops leaving for the Front Line from Victoria Station.

29

The Worcestershire Regiment march towards battle.

more than ten miles in either direction in the next three years.

The truth of trench warfare was that strategy and the way in which generals thought had parted company with the weaponry of war. Foch once wrote that "to make war means always attacking" and most other commanders seemed to follow this philosophy. But the weapons were primarily defensive in this period, and the previous method of delivering a fast attack, the cavalry charge, was outdated and impotent. Barbed wire, forts and trenches, machine-gun posts, supplies brought up by train or truck, heavy artillery and millions of men forced into fighting—these could stop an attack more easily than they could sustain one, and until a new "cavalry-horse" could be invented, a mechanical, man-carrying, death-delivering beast of the land or of the air, the generals could do no more than send their men to valiant but vain death.

It is traditional to divide the First World War into "battles"—the battle of the Marne, the battle of Ypres, and so on—but this is misleading. There was no peace between the battles apart from one very limited and poignant occasion; there was merely less shelling, less pressure, less concentration of misery, terror and death. Death came in many guises; it came with the exploding noise of the shell or the mortar bomb, or with

A painting of an English charge at Laon. Gas masks add an even more ghastly touch.

the drumbeat of the machine-gun or the rattle of the rifle; it came from the visible enemy with his grenade or bayonet, or it came in an eerie silence from a hidden foe, in the form of a fog of unstoppable greenish-yellow gas; it came from disease and it came from loss of blood; for many, it came because they had lost the will to survive in a man-made hell, and for a few, it came when they were executed by their fellow-soldiers for trying to run from the field of battle.

Gas was used at the second battle of Ypres in April 1915. The Germans had nearly 6,000 cylinders of chlorine with which they wanted to experiment, and they had to wait ten days until the wind blew in the right direction for them. They struck terror into the hearts of the French victims of the attack, and opened up a four mile gap in the front until fresh Canadian troops plugged it. But neither here, nor in the later assaults in this area of Artois, nor in the Champagne region to the south-east, did the lines of trenches shift more than three miles in 1915.

1916 saw the same pattern repeated, but on a larger and bloodier scale. The "battles" were Verdun and the Somme. The struggle for Verdun, the most famous and morale-boosting French fortress, began when a shell fired by a German fifteen-inch gun twenty miles away exploded in the middle of the

Big Bertha—a costly and overrated German weapon.

fortifications. The date was February 21st and between then and December 18th, about 420,000 men were killed, and a further 800,000 were gassed or wounded. Battle statistics became so big that they became unreal. The Germans had thirteen of their heaviest guns—"Big Berthas" as they were called—firing shells that weighed over a ton each; each gun needed twelve wagons to transport it. They had high velocity guns, whose shell arrived at the same time as the sound of it. They had hundreds of little field-guns, nick-named "Whizz-bangs" which lobbed shells into the trenches. On one day they fired 100,000 shells filled with a new gas into Verdun. As for the French, they were supplied with 4,000 tons of materials and 15,000 fresh troops every day, by 3,000 lorries churning along a single main road. Numbers became meaningless. "Most of my regiments stay in line for eight to twelve days, and only lose 30%" wrote a French General. In the end, the French pushed forward again. In October, using 150 aircraft as well as 700 guns, they recaptured land lost in February; in December they advanced again and took 11,000 prisoners, and the Germans allowed the battle to peter out.

On the Somme, the battle started on July 1st. At precisely 7.30 a.m., eleven British divisions rose out of their trenches and dugouts to attack the Germans. By nightfall they had lost 57,770 officers and men, most of them within a few hundred yards of their starting point. The village of Thiepval, which, according to the plans should have been captured by 7.45 a.m. on that first day, finally fell to the British on the eighty-ninth day of the battle, which eventually lasted for 141 days, and gained nine miles of useless land, at the cost of about half a million men on each side. Only one new thing came in the final phase of the battle, and that almost passed unrecognised: it was the use of a new weapon called, tentatively, the "tank".

Haig had ordered 150 of these experimental vehicles in April; 49 were delivered in early September, but 17 of these were useless because of mechanical failures. In the event, only 13 found their way onto the battlefield at the same time, where they were briefly very effective, even though "When our men first saw these strange creatures lolloping along the roads and over old battlefields, taking trenches on the way, they shouted and cheered wildly, and laughed for a day afterwards". Even the German High Command laughed at the novelty, which meant that when tanks appeared in force at the Battle of Cambrai on the 20th November 1917, the element of surprise was savagely strong. 378 tanks, 289 aircraft, and a barrage from 1,000 guns blasted through the strongest part of the German defences, the "Hindenburg Line" which the Germans had dug out behind the

Devastation near Verdun, 1916.

The First World War affected the whole population in an unprecedented way. Its cost in terms of human lives was so great that every effort to obtain volunteer soldiers was outrun by the casualty figures, and in 1916 Asquith's government compelled all males between the ages of 18 and 41 to be eligible for military service. The most famous poster of the war appealed to patriotism, and was highly successful. Even Lloyd George, who seldom had any words of praise for the Secretary of War, had to admit that 'Kitchener makes a great poster'. Not all the posters were so heroic in tone. Some appealed to fear and to self-interest, like the example below right; such were usually withdrawn quickly.

Posters were the main method of informing the general public, or of appealing for cooperation, and many of them emphasised the need for savings to pay the huge material costs. 'Invest in the War Loan today' was a familiar message, but it was given a fresh impact by the patriotic pun in the words 'The British Sovereign will win'.

DON'T IMAGINE YOU ARE NOT WANTED

EVERY MAN between 19 and 38 years of age is WANTED!

Ex-Soldiers up to 45 years of age

"YOUR COUNTRY NEEDS **YOU**"

MEN CAN ENLIST IN THE NEW ARMY FOR THE DURATION OF THE WAR

RATE OF PAY: Lowest Scale 7s. per week with Food, Clothing &c., in addition

1. **Separation Allowance for Wives and Children of Married Men when separated from their Families** (Inclusive of the allotment required from the Soldier's pay of a maximum of 6d. a day in the case of a private)

For a Wife **without** Children	- -	12s. 6d. per week
For Wife with One Child	-	15s. 0d. per week
For Wife with Two Children	-	17s. 6d. per week
For Wife with Three Children	-	20s. 0d. per week
For Wife with Four Children	-	22s. 0d. per week

and so on, with an addition of 2s. for each additional child.

Motherless children 3s. a week each, exclusive of allotment from Soldier's pay

2. **Separation Allowance for Dependants of Unmarried Men.**

Provided the Soldier does his share, the Government will assist liberally in keeping up, within the limits of Separation Allowance for Families, any regular contribution made before enlistment by unmarried Soldiers or Widowers to other dependants such as mothers, fathers, sisters, etc.

YOUR COUNTRY IS STILL CALLING. FIGHTING MEN! FALL IN!!

Full Particulars can be obtained at any Recruiting Office or Post Office.

Nº 0200
DAVID ALLEN & SONS Lᵈ
HARROW
LONDON

The battle of the Somme, 1916. One soldier keeps watch while his companions snatch sleep while and wherever they can.

main lines of fighting during the winter of 1916–17. To this they had deliberately fallen back in the spring of 1917, thereby ruining all the French plans for that year's attack on the centre of the German line, but they were still caught out at Cambrai.

Such success was sorely needed, for in the third battle of Ypres (July 31st–November 12th 1917), often referred to as Passchendaele, the British Army had started with great optimism, and had seen their hopes sink slowly in the mud of Flanders and the futility of the old discredited tactics. In March 1917 Canadian troops had won a brilliant victory at Vimy Ridge. In June the German fortifications on the Messines Ridge had disintegrated with a noise that was heard in London, when a million pounds of high explosive, placed 100 feet under the surface in nineteen secretly dug mines, were simultaneously detonated. But those spectacular triumphs could not bolster the Allies for ever. Many French troops mutinied in the summer of 1917, and British casualties were still horrifyingly high; there were nearly a quarter of a million officially listed for the period of Passchendale. And everywhere there was mud, clogging, clinging mud, churned up by the shells and increased by the highest autumn rainfall in living memory. In that clay plain of Flanders, trenches became drains, roads became marshes, shell-craters became lakes. There was no escape, and, it seemed, no future, unless the victory

An irony of war; a horse-drawn water cart bogged down in the Flanders mud.

at Cambrai meant something. The winter of 1917–18 was one of deepest despair.

The Germans too were desperate, and decided on a last great gamble. While British politicians were becoming sensitive about the casualty figures, and while the French army was still rebuilding its self-confidence, and before the Americans could send too many fresh troops to the Western Front, the German High Command resolved upon a giant offensive, with everything depending on its success. In March, April, May and July, the Germans crashed through the defensive lines in front of them. All the territory which the Allies had won at Passchendaele was snatched back; the ground gained at Cambrai had already been nibbled away, and the Germans swept over the River Aisne, and came back to the Marne, and crossed it. They were closer to Paris than they had ever been; they were back at the point where the Schlieffen plan had come adrift; they were back at the point where their troops outran their supplies and their organisation.

On July 18th, 1918, the French counterattacked, while Foch coordinated the plans of all the Allied leaders. The Australian commander Monash had been experimenting with tanks in battle, and discovered that four carrier-tanks could take forward loads which would have needed 1,250 men; he had also used aircraft to supply the front line. On August 8th, the first battle of

Facing page:
British troops resting just behind the lines.

Left:
An early tank in action on the Western Front.

a new era was fought at Amiens, when the mechanical skills and technological advances of the Allies were used in a way which spelled the end of trench warfare. 800 aircraft, 324 heavy tanks, 96 lighter fighting tanks, 120 supply tanks and 2,000 guns swept forward against the heaviest German resistance, carrying Australian, Canadian, French and British troops eight miles into the enemy lines, achieving almost all objectives by the middle of the day. It was the greatest German defeat of the war. They fell back, first through the mud of the main Western Front battle lines, then to their own Hindenburg Line. They were chased primarily by the British Third Army, who despite appalling casualties of over 300,000 men killed or wounded between August 8th and November 11th, harassed and hounded the Germans to defeat after defeat. Old patterns of problems appeared: the closer the Germans got to their homeland, the more stubbornly they resisted and the more difficult it was for the Allies to maintain their supply lines, but it was clear that the Germans could do no more than save what they could from the wreckage of the Western Front. The politicians were seeking an armistice; the German Navy mutinied at Kiel; the Kaiser abdicated on November 9th; the armistice delegates were told to sign whatever terms were offered to them.

On November 11th, Canadian members of the British Fifth Army re-entered Mons, the town near which the B.E.F. had joined battle fifty age-long months before. There they received the message that they most wanted: "Hostilities will cease at 11 hours today, November 11th . . ." Peace; calm, rest and stillness; an audible silence blanketed the Western Front for the first time in four years.

The sudden cessation of chaos brought to mind the one strange incident in 1914 when war had been buried by men instead of men by war. On Christmas Day, 1914, after a night in which the British soldiers in the front line near Armentières could hear the Germans singing carols on the other side of "No-Mans-Land", men of both sides lifted their heads above the protective parapets of the trenches, and with increasing confidence moved slowly into the open. Tentatively they came together. Wary eyes watched for treachery until at last they had trust in each other. They conversed as best they could, and exchanged possessions; cigarettes from the British, short cigars from the Germans, tins of bully beef, sausages. They relaxed, smiled, laughed. A German trooper ran back to his lines to fetch a camera, and they posed for group photographs. Then they became shy again. Slowly they separated, and drifted back to their own mud dugouts. There was no shooting for the rest of that day, and when it did start again, the shots of both sides were aimed deliberately, uselessly high. Within a few days, both sets of troops were moved by their commanders from that section of the line. In a war that could encompass twelve million deaths, there was no place for individual friendships across the front lines.

Strange faces of mercy: a French ambulance dog finds a wounded man . . .
. . . and an American nurse emerges from a front line casualty station.

Souvenir from France. This postcard was sent to England by a soldier awaiting his own return home. It held a few poppy petals in the pocket under the flap on which were embroidered the flags of the Allies, in the shapes of the numerals.

CHAPTER FOUR

By Land, Sea and Air   1914–1918

Great Britain suffered just over three quarters of a million men killed in the First World War. The British Empire lost a further quarter of a million. Germany lost two million soldiers, and nearly one million civilians. Russia lost at least 1,700,000 soldiers killed, two million civilians killed, and well over five million soldiers and civilians wounded. These last figures are a searing reminder that, however much we remember the war for its ghastly character on the Western Front, it was a *world* war. None of those Russians died on the Western Front, nor did any Turks or Rumanians or Serbs, or Japanese and Chinese whose countries declared war on Germany in 1914 and 1917 respectively. There were many other theatres of war besides that in Western Europe, some directly involving British interests and some being largely irrelevant to the issue of the duel of the European giants.

Most relevant and most costly of these other arenas was that known as the Eastern Front, where Russia faced the might of both Austria and Germany. Knowing that these were her two most probable enemies, she had evolved two mobilisation plans: Plan A, for war against Austria, and Plan G for war against Germany. It was Plan A that the Tsar hesitantly initiated at the end of July 1914; Austria was the primary enemy, and on September 6th 1914, the day on which the Germans were finally held on the Marne not far from Paris, the Russians were pressing the Austrians to defeat at Lemborg, in the Austrian province of Galicia. It was a notable victory, costing the Austrians 350,000 men and an area full of valuable oilwells. But the Russians simultaneously made the mistake of answering an appeal from the French to put part of Plan G into operation, by attacking westwards into Eastern Prussia, thereby putting pressure on Germany to take men away from the Western Front. The Russian response was utterly loyal to the Allies, and disastrously incompetent. Two armies moved westward, one of them having plenty of compasses but not a single map of the area into which they were moving. The commanders of the armies, Rennenkampf and Samsonov, were not on speaking terms with each other, and

41

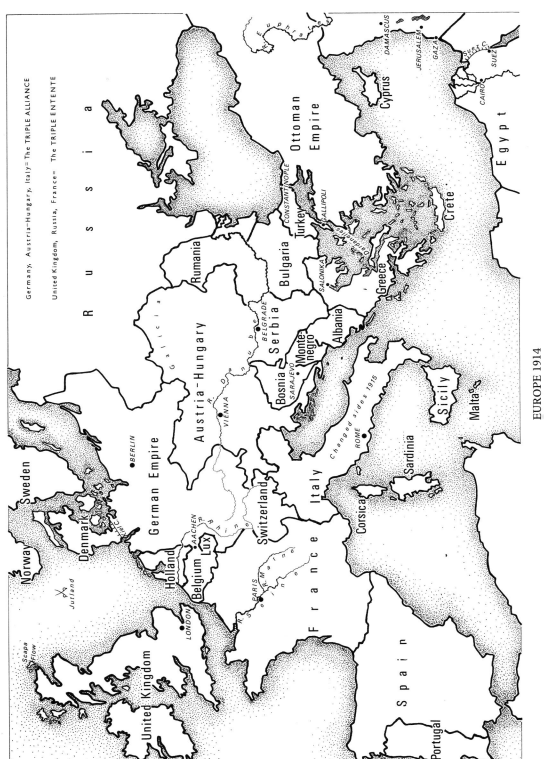

Germany, Austria-Hungary, Italy = The TRIPLE ALLIANCE

United Kingdom, Russia, France = The TRIPLE ENTENTE

EUROPE 1914

refused to communicate properly. When Rennenkampf won an easy but small victory on August 20th 1914, Samsonov decided that he could now rush ahead towards the heart of Germany. But on August 22nd the Germans brought out of retirement the sixty-seven year old General von Hindenburg, and gave him as his Chief of Staff General von Ludendorff, a younger and equally brilliant commander. Together they travelled to the Eastern Front, and concentrated on pushing back the flanks of Samsonov's advance, allowing his centre to come on. On August 30th and 31st, the Russian flanks were totally destroyed, and the centre was encircled. Ninety thousand Russians were taken prisoner, and Samsonov only avoided capture by hiding in a wood and finally committing suicide. This battle of Tannenberg was a heavy defeat for the Russians. Rennenkampf's army had to withdraw, losing 30,000 prisoners as it did so, and the Germans were now free to give support to their Austrian allies.

The Austrians were a feeble fighting force. At the beginning of the war they had occupied the Serbian capital, Belgrade, which was a few miles from their own frontier, but within a fortnight, the tiny Serbian army had thrust them back. Some of the German officers said that having Austria as an ally was like being "fettered to a corpse", and certainly the Russians, for all their own difficulties and confusions, were able to kick the "corpse" further back towards the Carpathian mountains and the plains of Hungary. But with considerable German stiffening and leadership, the Austrians advanced again in 1915, regaining all of Galicia and moving on into Poland (a Russian province). In the autumn of 1915 the line stabilised, but in March 1916 the Russians again showed their loyalty to the Allies by launching a huge attack against the Germans in order to relieve the pressure on Verdun. The line scarcely moved; the Russians lost five men for every one German that they killed, but even so, they responded to yet another appeal for help. Italy had by this time joined the war against her former allies Germany and Austria, and was hard pressed by the latter. Would the Russians please

43

attack in Galicia once more, to split the Austrian forces? Under
General Brusilov, one of the few outstanding generals of the
whole war, the Russians came forward. They captured 400,000
prisoners and 500 guns. This success encouraged Rumania to
declare herself on the Allies' side, and so the southern part of the
Eastern front looked from the German point of view as if it was
crumbling away. Again, they sent rapid reinforcements; again
they were triumphant as the Russian offensive petered out and
Rumania fell into their hands. Imperial Russia had sacrificed two
million casualties in 1915 and another million in 1916, and had
achieved nothing for herself. In March 1917, internal strains
caused the Tsar to abdicate, and although Brusilov led one more
great offensive in the summer of that year, in November Lenin
and the Communist party took power and sued for peace. In
March 1918, the Russians signed the Treaty of Brest-Litovsk,
which ended their part in the war against Germany.

There were three other main theatres of war on land, all against
the German ally Turkey, who managed to occupy two and a half
million British and Empire troops as well as French and Russians.
One was in Mesopotamia, the land between the rivers Tigris and
Euphrates, where British and Indian troops attacked the Turks in
order to protect the oil installations to the north of the Persian
Gulf. Victorious in 1915, the British became overconfident, and
had to surrender 10,000 men in Kut in 1916, before a more
methodical advance brought success in the capture of Baghdad in
1917.

The second "Middle Eastern" front was in Egypt and Palestine
and in the western deserts of Arabia. The Turks had hopes of
capturing the vital waterway of the Suez Canal, though they were
remarkably slow when war first broke out in organising their
attack. By December 1914, the minute British garrison on the
Canal had been reinforced by ANZAC men, soldiers of the
Australian and New Zealand Army Corps, and by English and
Indian troops from India. In the autumn of 1916, these troops
went onto the attack, moving across the Sinai desert towards

Lawrence of Arabia—
an informal photograph.

Palestine, building a pipeline as they did so to bring them fresh water from the Nile. Twice they were repulsed at Gaza by Turkish and German forces, and the English general, Murray, was replaced by General Allenby. He went straight into the front line himself, to raise the morale of the weary and pessimistic troops, and he also brought belated recognition and help to the work of the most romantic and legendary figure of the First World War, an Oxford graduate and member of the British Museum archaeological team excavating Carchemish on the Euphrates, T. E. Lawrence.

This young man had been in the Middle East for four years when war broke out, and he had come to know and admire the Arab temperament. The Arabs were proud and unwilling subjects of the Turks, and in 1916 when they started to rebel, unsuccessfully, Lawrence was an Intelligence officer based on Cairo. But he perceived that the Arabs had the right and the ability to achieve their freedom, and that its achievement would also help the Allied cause. Late in 1916 he was given permission to go to help the Arabs, and from then until the end of the war he became a flitting figure, appearing out of the desert, disrupting the Turks where they least expected it, and disappearing before they could take action against him. He encouraged the Arab revolt, but did not make the fatal mistake of trying to over-

45

organise it. His was an irregular, guerilla campaign. Not for him the bloody confrontation; he preferred the lightning raid, cutting the main railway line of Turkish communication, looping round to attack their rear, capturing the port of Aqaba from the landward side when the Turks expected attack from the sea, spreading revolt by putting heart into the Arabs and despair into the Turks.

With Lawrence thus occupying the attention of the Turks in the desert, Allenby could now attack the Gaza area again (1917). By feint attacks and by letting the Turks get hold of false plans for an attack on Gaza itself, he deceived them into an unbalanced defence. A sudden attack at Beersheba turned the Turkish flank, and Gaza fell two days later. On December 9th, 1917, Allenby entered Jerusalem, leading his striking white horse rather than riding it in triumph, a quaint gesture of humility from the first Christian general to capture the Holy City from the Moslems in six hundred years. In 1918 Allenby and Lawrence "of Arabia" raced for Damascus. Lawrence got there first, on October 1st 1918, while Allenby was fighting three Turkish armies with superb brilliance. This was a cavalry operation, and an outstanding one, one of the last in history, and the major cause of Turkey's surrender on October 30th.

The third front against the Turks was the most controversial one, the Dardanelles campaign of 1915, which was originally undertaken as a response to a Russian request to split the Turkish forces. The idea of attacking Turkey and threatening Constantinople received strong support from Winston Churchill, the First Lord of the Admiralty, Lord Kitchener, the Secretary for War, and Lord Fisher, the First Sea Lord. With backing like this, a plan to land on the Gallipoli peninsula and thus to force an opening through the Dardanelles should have been highly effective, especially as Turkey had only a few outdated forts and two divisions of ill-armed men guarding the area at the beginning of 1915. But nearly everything went wrong. The British War Council changed its plans and its priorities several times, and

Gallipoli: the Allies land at 'ANZAC' beach, piling their stores on the tiny beach, and pitching their tents precariously on the exposed hillside.

illness, ignorance and incompetence undermined most of the efforts in the vital area itself.

At first the War Council decided on a purely naval attack, so on February 19th an Anglo-French force of eight aged battleships and two modern ones began bombarding the Turkish forts. As days and weeks passed, slow progress was made against shore batteries and mines until on March 19th, eighteen allied ships were ready to attack "the Narrows", where the Dardanelles are less than a mile wide. Three ships struck mines and went to the bottom; three more were seriously disabled by gunfire, and the remainder withdrew, not knowing that at that moment the Turks had run out of shells, and that the way to Constantinople was open.

The naval attack having apparently failed, the War Council now resolved upon a military landing, an idea that they had been playing with for about a month. They forgot the warnings of a prewar study of the Gallipoli Peninsula, that in any attack "secrecy and surprise were essential", and went ahead with a plan for a landing on April 25th. The military attack was well handled, but the Turks and their German advisers had by now had two months warning, and six divisions of troops in well prepared positions awaited the invaders when the main British force came ashore on five separate beaches. Two beaches were

HMS *Dreadnought* in fighting trim.

complete death-traps; two were less well-covered by Turkish fire, but the troops made no advance inland. The remaining beach was undefended, but the Allies were forced out by a quick counter-attack. Meanwhile a flank attack by ANZAC units got a thousand yards inland, but failed to reach the necessary high ground where they could establish themselves. For the next three and a half months, trench warfare developed as immovably as it had on the Western Front, but with dysentery and other diseases striking down even more troops than the Turks were able to incapacitate. By July, the Turks had fifteen divisions in the area, and the Allies had increased their total to twelve.

In August, another landing and an assault on the high ground were attempted. As the troops neared the end of a difficult night march, they were shelled by their own ships, who mistook them for the enemy. The last opportunity of breaking through was ruined, and in two phases the expedition was evacuated. By the time the last man left the tip of the Peninsula in January 1916, 200,000 casualties had been suffered, by disease and enemy action, and there could be pride only in the gallantry of failure, and the efficiency of the evacuation by sea.

Rivalry on the sea had been one of the main issues between Germany and Britain before the war had broken out, but the story of the naval war is not the one which must have been foreseen by the builders of the Dreadnoughts. There was only one major confrontation between the British Grand Fleet and the German High Seas Fleet, which was in most respects indecisive though it produced some unpleasant and unforeseen results for Britain.

In July 1914, the British fleet assembled at Portland for a practice mobilisation. By the time the exercise was over, the Archduke Franz Ferdinand was dead, and the six week slide to war was gathering speed. The Navy was therefore kept at battle stations, and unlike its German rival was ready for action as soon as war was declared. The German High Seas Fleet seemed unready and unwilling to come out of its heavily fortified sanctuaries in the Baltic, and the British found themselves fulfilling a traditional role, blockading the Continent and cutting off maritime trade with Germany. There was one minor battle in the North Sea at Heligoland Bight in late August, when four German ships were sunk, and shortly before this the B.E.F. had been transported to France so efficiently that the Germans were unaware of its passage. Later in the year, three British cruisers were sunk in a day by one submarine, and twice the east coast of England was bombarded by German cruisers. A third similar raid was intercepted in early 1915, however, and the Germans never tried again.

Elsewhere in the world, Britain started the war badly. Two German ships bombarded French bases on the North African coast, and shortly afterwards sailed past the British Mediterranean Fleet. The date was August 4th, 1914, but because the declaration of war did not come into effect until midnight, the German ships were allowed to escape to Turkey, where their presence helped to persuade the Turks to join the war on the German side. Two German cruisers in the Atlantic sank twenty two British merchant ships in August before they were destroyed, and the German cruiser *Emden* slipped from the Pacific into the Indian Ocean and enjoyed a remarkable career before being outgunned and driven onto a reef by the Australian

49

cruiser *Sydney* in November 1914. In the previous 79 days the *Emden* had sunk or captured twenty four ships, including thirteen ships in a fortnight in the Bay of Bengal and a Russian cruiser and a French destroyer in Penang harbour. She had also called at the remote British Islands of Diego Garcia, which had not heard of the outbreak of war and so happily provisioned the ship; she set fire to a half-million ton fuel depot near Madras; and by putting up a dummy funnel had confused everyone as to which ship she actually was. Before the end, seventy eight British ships were hunting the seas for her.

The other German naval success in 1914 was at the Battle of Coronel, off the Chilean coast, where the only powerful flotilla of German ships outside German harbours caught and destroyed a smaller British squadron. It was a humiliating defeat, resulting in the dismissal of the British First Sea Lord, Prince Louis of Battenberg, and the appointment of the pugnacious John Fisher. Six weeks later, when the German flotilla under Admiral von Spee arrived at the British Falkland Islands to destroy the wireless station there, they found a total of seven cruisers waiting for them, including the *Invincible* and the *Inflexible*. Four of the five German ships went down, fighting to the last possible moment; the British suffered only thirty casualties, which was twenty eight more than the Germans had suffered at Coronel.

A total of twelve ships fought at the Falkland Islands. In the only remaining—and the only major—confrontation between the navies, two hundred and fifty nine surface vessels were involved, a clash of giants that was never to be repeated. In May 1916, the German Admiral decided to try to lure the British Grand Fleet to destruction. His plan was to send his battle-cruiser squadron openly into the North Sea, while sixteen submarines were to ambush the Grand Fleet as it came out of harbour. The High Seas Fleet would then pick off the survivors of the underwater attack. What developed was the Battle of Jutland, and it took a form which followed nobody's plan.

The lurking submarines had no effect on the Grand Fleet; in

A German painting of the return from Jutland. Sailors scramble down the sloping sides of their sinking cruiser, while other ships stand by to pick them up, and a Zeppelin gives support from the air.

fact, Admiral Jellicoe was totally unaware that they had ever been there. Patchy visibility, the absence of efficient air reconnaissance, and appalling signalling by the British ships almost prevented any contact at all between the fleets. It was only because a British light cruiser went off course to investigate a neutral Danish steamer that a German light cruiser was sighted doing the same thing. Their firing attracted the heavier ships, and by mid-afternoon on May 31st 1916, squadrons of British and German battle-cruisers, led by Admirals Beatty and Hipper respectively, opened fire on each other at a range of ten miles. By half past four, the *Indefatigable* and the *Queen Mary* had been hit in their ammunition magazines, exploded and sunk with enormous loss of life, and the battle was going Germany's way, but a new phase was coming as the Dreadnoughts of both Jellicoe and Scheer raced towards the heart of the battle. Visibility was worsening as the smoke of more than two hundred and fifty ships wafted over the sea; the British suffered frequently by being silhouetted against the brighter western sky. Identification of vessels was difficult as they came towards each other at closing speeds of up to 45 knots, but what was happening was that Scheer and the German Dreadnoughts were heading into the iron jaws of the British Grand Fleet. Isolated actions were going on elsewhere: the light cruiser *Chester* was being pounded into helplessness by a total of five German ships while Jack Cornwell, Boy 1st Class, stood by his useless gun turret awaiting orders although he had been mortally wounded at the beginning of the action. He was one of three recipients of the Victoria Cross in this action, and remains the youngest ever to receive Britain's highest award for gallantry.

The main battle fleets were in contact for twenty minutes only, before Scheer realised his danger and turned south and then unexpectedly west to avoid further action. In those twenty minutes, Admiral Hood's flagship *Invincible* suddenly blew up, broke in two, and disappeared beneath the waves. Only six survivors of her crew of 1,026 men were found. Jellicoe searched for Scheer in the failing light and found him. Heavy damage was inflicted on the German ships, and Scheer ordered a mass torpedo attack, but the range was too great and the torpedo tracks were spotted in plenty of time for the British to take evasive action, a manoeuvre which cost them no casualties but caused them to lose contact with Scheer again. Although at 8.15 in the evening, Beatty signalled to Jellicoe to tell him where the Germans were, Jellicoe refused to follow up that moment lest he should be tricked onto mines or into another torpedo attack. He was, as Churchill said, the only man who could lose the war in a single afternoon, and he was not prepared to risk Britain's control of the seas. By the morning, the German fleets had vanished, and it was time to count the cost.

So confused had the battle been that it was only now that Jellicoe became aware of the loss of the *Indefatigable* and the *Queen Mary*, and at first sight, Britain had fared badly. Fourteen ships had sunk, including three highly prized battle cruisers; no equivalent German ship had been seen to go down, though one did sink on the way back from the battle, and ten smaller German vessels had been destroyed. Over six thousand British sailors had lost their lives.

Who won? The British suffered the greater damage, and their armour was shown to be as ineffective as their armour-piercing shells; their signalling too had not been adequate. But on June 2nd, thirty-six hours after the battle, Jellicoe signalled to the Admiralty that he was ready to put to sea. Scheer's High Seas Fleet never came out in force again, until it sailed to Scapa Flow in November 1918, to surrender itself, and as a final gesture to scuttle itself in the dark and icy water. Britannia could claim still to rule the waves.

What was happening beneath the waves was a different story. Britain had entered the war with more submarines than the Germans (thirty-six to twenty-eight), but the Germans were more aware of the potential of this new weapon and increased its production rapidly. In 1915 they began to sink all merchant and neutral shipping. The Cunard liner *Lusitania* was sunk in May, with the loss of nearly 1,200 lives, many of them American. Political pressure from this neutral country was so strong that the Germans limited their "U-boat" campaign to attacks against declared enemies, until in February 1917 they once again announced unrestricted submarine warfare, in the hope of starving Britain of food and raw materials. It was a policy of desperation which nearly succeeded, like the great final offensive on the Western Front in 1918. One ship in every four that left British ports in April 1917 failed to return. One million tons of British and neutral shipping were destroyed in that month, ten times more than could be replaced in the same time by fresh launchings. Foreign crews refused to sail to British waters, and the stocks of wheat in Britain dwindled to enough to feed the population for six weeks only. Mines, zig-zagging, depth charges and Q-ships (armed ships disguised as merchantmen) all produced some successes in sinking U-boats, but only the convoy system, ordered by the Prime Minister Lloyd George against the advice of the Admiralty, actually brought down the rate of sinkings. Merchant ships were organised into massive fleets with destroyer protection, and of the 88,000 ships that travelled in convoy between May 1917 and November 1918, only 456 were sunk. Although the Germans had 140 U-boats in operation in October 1917, they could not break down the protective system, and by the end of the year American and British shipyards were beginning to build ships as fast as they were being lost at sea. The threat of total war in a new dimension had been overcome in the nick of time, and heroic attacks on U-boat bases at Zeebrugge and Ostend in 1918 reduced the menace still further.

War under the sea was not the only new menace. War in, or from, the air had become a reality. Balloons had been used for aerial spotting in the Boer War by the British, but it was the French, with Bleriot as their inspiration, who thought of using heavier-than-air machines for artillery control and recon-naissance, and the Germans who pioneered the airship under the

A British squadron in flight over France.

guidance of an ex-cavalry man, Count Zeppelin. The British cavalry objected to the use of aeroplanes at first, because the noise upset their horses. Besides, they could not understand how these string and canvas affairs could be useful in wartime, when they were so vulnerable to engine failure, bad weather and being shot down. The Royal Flying Corps was founded, against opposition, in 1912, and four squadrons flew to France in August 1914, sixty-three aircraft out of one hundred and thirteen in Britain. Germany had three times as many, and thirty airships.

The war in the air had no decisive impact on the result of the First World War. It was the other way round; the First World War had a decisive impact on war in the air, by indicating what could happen, and just how aeroplanes and airships could be used. England was bombed by both types of weapon; less than a thousand civilians were killed, but it was a sign of things to come. In 1914, bombs were dropped over the side of flimsy craft by the navigators; by 1918, Britain had developed night bombers which could carry sixteen 112-pound bombs, and stay aloft for eight hours. All sorts of specialised craft developed, such as fighters, spotter planes, transports and bombers, and in 1917 the Royal Air Force was brought into existence in recognition of a new and vital development. By the end of the war the R.A.F. had 22,000 aircraft and 300,000 men. The stage was already being set for the new

A German drawing illustrating the unsophisticated nature of war in the air. One officer is about to drop a bomb on an artillery 'spotter' balloon, while the other uses a rifle to fight off a French monoplane.

type of war which would be acted out in the German "blitzkrieg" in 1939 and the Battle of Britain in 1940.

The air war was the one place in 1914–1918 where individuals stand out. The men involved were relatively few, and the style of combat like an old-fashioned duel. Each side had its "aces", the greatest being the Baron von Richthofen, who shot down eighty Allied planes before he was himself shot down and killed. Such was the British respect for him that they dropped a wreath and a message behind the enemy lines: "Rittmeister Baron Manfred von Richthofen was killed in aerial combat on April 21st, 1918. He was buried with full military honours. From the British Royal Air Force". It was not a boastful deed, but a symbol of the bond of understanding that aerial fighters had for each other. The dogfights above the sticky mud of Flanders were individual affairs, where a man grew to know his enemy before he killed or was killed.

One last "front" remains to be mentioned, the so-called "Home Front". The Great War was not confined to the areas of direct conflict only, but had to be "fought" by civilian populations too. For the first time in British history, compulsory military service was instituted, and those who would not fight for reasons of conscience often found themselves in the thickest parts of the battles, as stretcher bearers. Other men were sent to vital jobs, in

Flying at Hendon, 1914. This is one of the many striking posters which were commissioned to encourage passengers to travel on London's public transport, and which remain excellent illustrations of the art and the style of the passing years.

Volunteer workers send library books to the men overseas.

the mines and in the munitions factories, and women were called upon to undertake work that previously had been considered suitable for men only. A largely voluntary rationing scheme was introduced as food became scarce. Taxes shot up; heavy duties were put on anything that might be considered a luxury good. Ships were commandeered by the Government, and an attempt was made to impose a "black-out". Suspected spies were locked up without trial, and anyone with a German sounding name was likely to be unpopular. The British Royal Family changed its name to Windsor from Saxe-Coburg, and Prince Louis of Battenberg translated his name to make it Mountbatten. Civilians endured the war with a mixture of horror and humour, patience and panic. They searched the evermounting casualty lists in the newspapers for the names of loved ones, and yet they laughed at themselves and at the enemy depicted in the cartoons. They put up with the shortages of material and the long hours of work, but they panicked when German bombs fell. They accepted the inevitability of what was going on, and they recognised above all that when the war was over, things would never be the same again. For no-one was this more true than for the women. They were losing a whole generation of husbands or brothers, sons or fathers, but they were also winning their own battle to be recognised as responsible citizens in the post-war world.

The history of British airships is full of disasters. After Count Zeppelin of Germany had successfully made several airships which appeared to have military and freight- and passenger-carrying capabilities, public opinion forced the British Government to authorise the Admiralty to construct the country's first airship. Designed to be larger than any other airship in the world, it was totally wrecked while being taken out of its hangar for its first flight in 1911. Britain's first operational airship appeared in 1917 when Germany had thirty in the air. In 1921, Britain sold her latest airship to the United States government; on its fourth test flight it broke in half in midair, killing the forty-four men on board, and Britain abandoned further developments until 1924. Two new ships were then designed, the R100 and the R101. The R100 flew to Canada and back in 1930, a highly successful flight. The R101 crashed on her maiden flight in France, killing forty-six people, including the Air Minister. R100 was scrapped, and Britain gave up the idea of lighter-than-air machines.

Airships were shown to be difficult to build and to control in the air, but they had a number of attractions. Their cabins, in a gondola attached to the bottom of the gas-filled balloon, were spacious and luxurious, and they offered accommodation that no aircraft and few liners could rival. They flew smoothly and quietly, and for vast distances, though they were slow; 50–60 m.p.h. was a good average speed, and so Atlantic crossings could be achieved faster than in a liner at sea. Airships were used to explore the Arctic, to cross all the major oceans of the world, to carry passengers and mail, and to fight, but other transport developments and the difficulties and dangers of controlling up to five million cubic feet of gas prevailed over Count Zeppelin's dream. Between 1859 (when Zeppelin made his first semi-rigid airship) and 1936, over 150 airships were built throughout the world. More than half of them met with disaster.

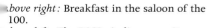

Above right: Breakfast in the saloon of the R100.
Above left: The R101 circling over St. Paul's.
Below right: The burnt-out wreckage of the R101, giving some idea of the scale of these vast vehicles.

CHAPTER FIVE

Unfinished Business   1901–1928

In 1903, Mrs Emmeline Pankhurst could certainly claim to be a responsible citizen. Widow of a former Liberal Member of Parliament and mother of two daughters, she was a well-educated and respectable person, a friend of many politicians and an intelligent and idealistic crusader. Her cause was one that had been raised from time to time ever since Mary Wollstonecraft had written a book called *Vindication of the Rights of Women* in 1792, the cause of the political and legal equality of women with men. Women in the nineteenth century were regarded as inferior beings: their property became the property of their husband alone when they married, and they could have no more control over it; they could be divorced, but could not divorce their husbands; they were not allowed, by social convention, to have any views on politics and business, and in order to get books accepted by publishers, some had to resort to pretending that they were males. Above all, however, they could not vote, and because they therefore could not influence the politicians who made the law of the land, they could see little likelihood of their situation changing. Not all women wanted it to change—Queen Victoria ironically was very much against any change in the role of "ordinary" women—but Mrs Pankhurst had married one of the few politicians who was prepared to speak out for "Votes for Women", and after his death she and her daughters devoted themselves to that cause.

In 1903 Mrs Pankhurst founded in her Manchester home the Women's Social and Political Union which aimed to publicise the case for women's rights. It was at first a peaceful group which held small private meetings and tried to convert other people to its views. It was too slow a process, and at the end of 1905, as the country prepared for the General Election which was to sweep the Liberals into power early in 1906, the women of the WSPU went into action. In similar demonstrations in Manchester and in London, they embarrassed the campaigning Liberals like Sir Henry Campbell-Bannermann (the Prime Minister), Sir Edward Grey (Foreign Secretary) and Winston Churchill by rising to their

Left: Mrs Pankhurst and her daughter Christabel in prison clothing, 1908.
Right: Arrested Suffragettes being led away after an attack on Buckingham Palace in 1914.

feet during question time in political meetings and asking "Will the Liberal Government give votes for women?". It was a question that few politicians dared answer in public, for they could not tell what reaction a positive or a negative answer would bring in the forthcoming election. Mute and red-faced, they sat unhappily on their platforms, until stewards had bundled the women out into the streets. But smuggled banners inscribed with slogans like "Votes for Women" or "Will the Liberal Government give justice to working-women?" were unfurled from galleries; little white flags were waved by daring supporters of the "Suffragettes"; and publicity abounded.

These women were not really breaking the law—yet; they were offending against the attitudes of the time. They chained themselves to railings outside No. 10 Downing Street and in the House of Commons, and they organised processions and public meetings. Many of them were arrested for "obstruction", or, if they struggled, for "assaulting the police", and they were generally fined between four shillings (20p) and a pound, with an alternative of going to prison for a short time if they failed to pay. They always chose to go to prison: it gave them more publicity,

61

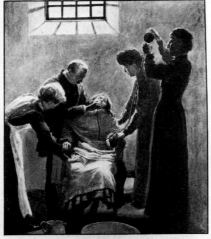

FORCIBLE FEEDING THROUGH THE NOSE OF WOMEN SUFFRAGIST PRISONERS.

This system is practised by our prison authorities owing to Women Suffragist Prisoners adopting the "Hunger Strike," which they have done, not to escape imprisonment, but to obtain the treatment previously accorded to political prisoners. "Woman Suffrage" is undoubtedly a political movement.

Forcible feeding—a poster designed to increase public sympathy for the women.

especially if they could arrange to get their arrest photographed by the Press. They were intent upon making the general public, male and female, think about the rights of women, and they were succeeding, and winning as much support as opposition.

But for some in the WSPU, the pace was still too slow. The movement split into the moderates and those demanding more action, and the latter inevitably attracted the newspaper headlines. Even the Pankhurst family became divided against itself. Sylvia Pankhurst began to lead an East-End-of-London social movement for working women's rights, while her mother Emmeline was either touring America or England trying to get support for the militants or was committing militant actions which caused her to be sent to prison, and her elder sister Christabel was directing such activities from Paris, where she was safe from arrest. Emmeline Pankhurst at first found it hard to break the law deliberately. Not only was she uncertain about the new tactics; she was also unable to throw very straight, and she had to practise in a friend's garden before attempting—unsuccessfully—to throw a stone through the window of No. 10 Downing Street. But she led demonstrations and window-smashing expeditions, and like hundreds of other suffragettes, she was more than once sent to prison. Pictures in the National Gallery were slashed, post boxes were set on fire, bombs were exploded, churches were burnt. Nothing was sacred any more.

Bitterness and confusion crept into the struggle. The women in prison refused to eat, and gave publicity to the horrors of being forcibly fed, a process involving the pushing of a rubber tube up the nose of the victim and then down the throat into the stomach, so that life-giving liquid could be poured into the "hunger-striker". Public opinion was revolted by this procedure. In 1913 the Government passed a cunning but again despised law which enabled prison authorities to release from gaol women whose life was seriously threatened by their voluntary starvation, and yet also enabled police officers to re-arrest those women as soon as their friends had nursed them back to health. This law was compared with the cruelty of a cat which catches and injures a mouse, and then lets it go in order to catch it again and again. The "Prisoners' Temporary Release Act" was soon known as the "Cat and Mouse Act", and although many politicians were angered and antagonised by the way the women were behaving, as were many voters, there grew up an increasing awareness of the life-and-death determination of the suffragettes to achieve their objectives.

In 1913, Miss Emily Davison darted from the crowd of race-goers at Tattenham Corner at Epsom as the Derby was being run, and threw herself under the horse owned by the King. She died of

A martyr's death: Emily Davison died after bringing down the King's horse in the 1913 Epsom Derby.

63

An unusually silent Suffragette march, at the funeral of Emily Davison.

her injuries a few days later, and six thousand women suffragettes marched in her funeral cortege. It symbolised the whole movement. The cause had its martyr; it had its own marching song, written by the composer Ethel Smyth, the woman who taught Emmeline Pankhurst to throw stones; it had its own sense of pride and courage and loyalty, and there seemed to be no solution unless the men in Parliament were prepared to give way. However the fanaticism of the women had frightened the Members of Parliament, and a private member's Bill to give the vote to women was rejected in late 1913. In June 1914, Mr Asquith, the Prime Minister, seemed to be convinced by the law-abiding Sylvia Pankhurst that women ought to have the vote, but there was no chance for him to show this publicly and turn the tide of opinion in the House. The Great War was only weeks away, and this struggle was to overwhelm all the other issues at home.

Nonetheless it broke the stalemate that had developed, for it put a new dignity into the women, and gave the men the chance to change their stand without losing face. Although initially the war meant the closing down of numerous mills and factories where women worked, and therefore a great increase in female unemployment, before long the huge casualty lists and the

Women getting training in what had been men's work, on the buses . . .

departure of more men to the front lines made it vital that women were used in the war effort. The weight of the WSPU was thrown into a new battle against the attitudes of men. In July 1915 Christabel Pankhurst personally led the last and the greatest demonstration, when thirty thousand women followed her down Whitehall with a slogan: "We demand the right to serve". Their leaders met Lloyd George, then the Minister for Munitions, and he promised that not only could they work in the munitions industry, but that they would receive a guaranteed minimum wage, and in many instances the same rate of pay as male workers. It was a crucial yet unspectacular revolution in the whole British way of life. Nearly $1\frac{1}{2}$ million more women were permanently employed in Britain in 1918 than had been at the outbreak of war; about seven million women had had jobs at some time during the war. The biggest single group were in the shells industry, making the weapons for their men to use against the enemy; they worked twelve hour shifts for seven days a week, but their conditions of health and safety were carefully supervised, so that after the war most factory workers found that their working life was improved.

The women took over the running of the London buses. They proved to be better than men at certain branches of engineering.

... and in the fire brigade.

They trained as plumbers and as electricians, and nearly a quarter of a million women entered Government service as secretaries and office workers. In 1917 they even joined the Army, when the Women's Army Auxiliary Corps was set up to help mainly with communications. They trained and drilled like men, a fact which necessitated the raising of their skirt hemlines to a whole twelve inches above the ground, in itself another revolution. Later the Women's Royal Naval Service and the Women's Royal Air Force were set up, altogether bringing the total of women in uniform to about 92,000.

By the end of the war, the "gentle sex" had clearly defeated the attitude that they were not responsible citizens. Just as the sacrifices of the soldiers had made it right that any man who was liable to be asked to die for his country had the right to vote for its government, so the efforts of the women had justified their inclusion in the law-making process. No-one seriously questioned the fact that women should be given the vote at once, except on mathematical grounds, for if all women and all men over the age of twenty-one were enfranchised, the total of female voters would be greater than that of the males. For this reason alone, the 1918 Representation of the People Act gave the vote to all men over 21 (except conscientious objectors who were disqualified for five years, and soldiers who had fought in the war who could vote at 19) and to all women over 30. None doubted that women would eventually be put on equal terms with men, and that moment was reached in 1928, when every adult except certified lunatics, felons in prison, members of the House of Lords and the Royal Family was granted at least one vote; some had two, a relic of past privilege which was finally removed in 1948.

In the end it was not the suffering that had brought the suffrage, but the work, the cooperation and the positive sacrifices that the war had demanded that had won the victory. Mrs Emmeline Pankhurst died in the year of final triumph, 1928; her daughters Christabel and Sylvia each lived to the age of 78, dying in 1958 and 1960 respectively, and always divided by their views on socialism and the rights of workers. It was a sad and bitter division, an unhappy postscript to the story, but a legacy of arguments early in the days of the WSPU.

Before, during and after the Great War, successive British Governments were faced by another legacy of division and bitterness which posed far greater problems of security and conscience than the Suffragettes had ever done. The tensions in the torn land of Ireland reached a new and terrible peak in the period 1912–1923, to which the war could not provide a face-saving solution.

Gladstone, who in the nineteenth century had done more to try to solve the Irish problem than any other politician, once compared the task with that of Sisyphus. This legendary figure, having incurred the anger of the gods, was condemned to spend his life rolling a boulder up to the pinnacle of a mountain. Each time he got to the top, the stone failed to balance and rolled down the other side and he had to start again; it was an ordeal without end. So seemed the efforts to bring peace and harmony to the people of Ireland, who had all been citizens of Great Britain since the Act of Union of 1800. This was an Act, however, which thinly papered over the cracks of racial, religious and political differences which threatened to cause the whole building of Britain to collapse. Ever since Elizabethan soldiers had been given the best lands in Ireland, and more especially since Oliver Cromwell had with his Puritan forces subjected the Irish Catholic natives to iron English rule, hatred had run deep. When King William III of Orange crushed the Irish Catholics at the Battle of the Boyne in 1690, and more Protestants from the mainland (including Scotland) came to keep order in Ireland, the stage was set for centuries of simmering strife, which was made worse by the terrible disaster of the Irish potato blight in 1845 and the resultant starvation and hardship for the peasants in 1846 and afterwards.

Gladstone's awareness of the tensions and his efforts to make laws to reduce them served only to focus attention on them and to increase the determination of the Irish to free themselves from English rule. It also divided English politicians bitterly, for when in 1886 and again in 1893 he introduced a bill to give Ireland the right to govern itself on all internal issues, he lost the support of many Liberal politicians who eventually joined with the Conservatives in their determination that "the Union" of England and Ireland should go on. These "Unionists" held a majority in the House of Lords in and after 1893, and so prevented any change in the status of Ireland. But in the early twentieth century, the situation changed dramatically.

First, the Liberals in the 1906 election and the two elections of 1910 tried to drop their Gladstonian commitment to "Home Rule" and concentrate on issues of social reform, the "People's Budget" and the reform of the House of Lords. (See Chapter 2). But second, the results of the 1910 elections meant that those same Liberals were utterly dependent on the votes of the Irish Nationalist party in Parliament if they wished to pass their Budget and their reform of the Lords. And third, once the Parliament Act of 1911 was passed and the Lords had lost their power of veto, the Irish Nationalists knew that the last obstacle to Home Rule had been overcome, and the price that they demanded for all the assistance that they had given to the Liberals was nothing less than freedom for their country from the power of the Parliament at Westminster. The Liberals could no longer pretend that they were not bound to support Home Rule, and in 1912, fully aware of the storms of protest that he would arouse, Asquith introduced a Home Rule bill into Parliament, very similar to that of Gladstone in 1893. The Lords, predictably, rejected it after it had passed the Commons. The same passage and rejection occurred again in 1913. According to the terms of the new Parliament Act, if the bill passed the Commons once more, it could go to the King for signature and thence onto the statute books whatever the Lords did or said.

But there was one further feature in the twentieth century struggle which had not appeared in Gladstone's time simply because while the House of Lords was powerful, there was no need for it. That new feature was the absolute determination of the Anglo-Irish Protestant men and women, living mainly in Ulster in the north-east of Ireland, not to be governed by the inevitably Irish Catholic majority who would under Home Rule set up the new government in Dublin. If the House of Lords could no longer save the Union, these Ulstermen would at least save themselves from becoming part of it, and they were fully supported by the Unionists in England. In July 1912, Bonar Law, leader of the Conservative and Unionist party, declared at a rally at Blenheim Palace "I can imagine no length of resistance to which Ulster can go in which I should not be prepared to support them, and in which, in my belief, they would not be supported by the overwhelming majority of the British people". It was a statement which hinted even at civil war, a possibility made more likely by the fact that Law and Sir Edward Carson, the leader of the Ulster Unionists in Parliament, had already attended a march-past of 100,000 "Ulster Volunteers" who during the course of 1912 became the nucleus of half a million Ulstermen who signed a covenant pledging their loyalty to George V while at the same time announcing their complete opposition to any attempt to

69

bring them under a Dublin parliament. By March 1914, when the Home Rule bill was being introduced for the third and final time in the House of Commons, it seemed possible that the British Army might be called upon to fight against Ulstermen whose only offence was that they wanted to stay British. The rock of Sisyphus had rolled a long way down the mountain again, and in doing so, it had dislodged other rocks, for it brought about what became misleadingly known as "the Curragh Mutiny".

The Curragh was the main British army camp in Ireland, near Dublin. Many of the soldiers there were Ulstermen, and they obviously had no desire to fight against their own people. The Commander-in-Chief in Ireland, Sir Arthur Paget, put this problem to the War Minister, John Seely, who told him that officers from Ulster could be allowed to "disappear" for a time, but that any other officers must obey all orders or be dismissed. Paget returned to Ireland to brief his officers, who got the impression that they had to choose between advancing north against Ulster or being dismissed. Fifty-eight of them promptly resigned their commissions. It was not a "mutiny" in the true sense, but in order to repair the damage and to get the officers to take up their posts again, Seely promised, without the authorization of the Cabinet, that the Army would not be used against Ulster. Asquith dramatically dismissed Seely, becoming War Minister himself.

There were other twists in the tale. Asquith offered any county in Ireland the right to vote itself out of Home Rule for six years, but this was just, as Carson put it, "a sentence of death with a stay of execution for six years", and he would not accept it. Asquith also banned the importation of arms to Ireland, but the Northern Irish Ulster Volunteers were successful in smuggling in 30,000 weapons and 3,000,000 rounds of ammunition whereas the Southern Irish Nationalists were prevented by the army and police from landing illegal arms in a harbour near Dublin. In July 1914, George V managed to persuade the leaders of all the major parties involved to meet in conference at Buckingham Palace to discuss the possible partition of Ireland into two parts, but no agreement could be reached on what were the true boundaries of Ulster, and the meeting broke up fruitlessly.

Again, the Great War intervened. Britain was mobilising against Germany within a fortnight of the end of the Buckingham Palace Conference, and although the third reading of the Home Rule bill passed in the Commons in September 1914, and the King signed it, it had already been agreed that the new law would not be put into operation until the war against Germany had been won. Briefly, there was a breathing space, and the Irish problem was put on one side. There it remained until 1916, when with little warning, rebellion broke out in Dublin.

The leader of the Irish Nationalist party at Westminster, John Redmond, was in terms of Irish politics a moderate man. He and most of his followers accepted the postponement of Home Rule, and indeed many Irishmen from the South as well as from Ulster volunteered to fight against Germany. This meant that leadership of the stubborn and fanatical anti-British struggle passed into the hands and mouths of more extreme men, like Arthur Griffith who had founded "Sinn Fein" (meaning "Ourselves Alone") in 1904, and James Connolly and Michael Collins who led an "Irish Citizen Army", and even a woman, Countess Markievicz, who combined nationalist with socialist motives for fighting the British. This group planned a rebellion for Easter Day, 1916, which they knew might be almost suicidal, but which might just bring about the great dream of Irish independence. Theoretically they had thousands of followers, although only perhaps 1,250 took part in the Rising.

The rebels hoped to receive arms from Germany, which was obviously likely to support any anti-British military movement. Sir Roger Casement, Irish-born but a former British consul who had accepted a knighthood from Queen Victoria, went to Germany from the neutral United States of America, and there tried to tempt Irish prisoners of war captured by the Germans to turn their coats and fight against the British; he also tried to

71

Left: Sir Roger Casement, executed for treason in 1916.

Right: Eamonn de Valera addressing a meeting in America, 1919.

persuade the German authorities to send arms to the Irish revolutionaries. He was largely unsuccessful, and on Good Friday 1916 he landed in Ireland from a German submarine with a warning that neither arms nor men would be available on Easter Day. The Royal Navy had however partly cracked the German naval code, and they were on the look-out for unusual activities. Casement was arrested shortly after he landed, and eventually tried for high treason, of which he claimed he could not be guilty as he was an Irishman, not an Englishman. He was nevertheless found guilty, and hanged on August 3rd, 1916.

The Easter Rising took place despite his failure and arrest. On Easter Monday, small groups of the Citizen Army and Sinn Fein marched through the wondering Bank Holiday crowds in the streets of Dublin, and seized various strongpoints within the city. Their headquarters, where they immediately proclaimed the creation of the provisional government of the new Irish Republic, was the General Post Office. They also seized the main Law Courts, a stadium called St Stephen's Green, a flour mill which overlooked the route by which British reinforcements might come, and about nine other buildings or groups of buildings. They failed to gain access to Dublin Castle, which was the British headquarters, but they cut most of the telephone wires, rendering the British High Command useless for a while.

If the ordinary Irishman had followed their lead, or if the Germans had taken them seriously, or if the British had lost the will to accept the challenge, then the Rising must have succeeded. As it was, none of these things happened, and inexorably, in the course of the next week, the Rising was cut down. Its leaders

Above: A painting of the scene inside the GPO in Dublin, just before its evacuation. Connolly lies on a stretcher, still giving orders.

Below: The ruined interior of the GPO after the Easter Rising.

knew that one way or another they must lose their lives, and they fought with fearless courage. On the Friday after Easter, James Connolly issued a Proclamation from the General Post Office:

"To Soldiers,

This is the fifth day of the establishment of the Irish Republic, and the flag of our country still floats . . . for the first time in 700 years . . . in Dublin City . . . As you know, I was twice wounded yesterday, and am unable to move about, but have got my bed moved into the firing line and . . . will be just as useful to you as ever."

But the rebels were outnumbered twenty to one, and the Post Office had been shelled and set on fire, and was burning from the top downwards. The rebels slipped into nearby houses while the army continued to shell the empty building, but on the Saturday, knowing that no further help was coming and that many innocent civilians were being shot and bayoneted simply because the army had no way of identifying its true enemies, the leaders surrendered themselves. They were rapidly tried by court martial, found guilty, and shot. Connolly, already dying from his wounds, had to be propped up in a chair to face the firing squad. Fifteen leaders of the Rising were executed, though Michael Collins escaped to fight on, and Eamonn De Valera, who had commanded the Volunteers at the flour mill, was eventually sentenced to life imprisonment rather than death; this was partly because of public dislike of the executions, and partly because he held an American passport, having been born of a Spanish father and an Irish mother in New York. Britain was understandably very conscious of American public opinion, for not only was America a major source of sympathy for the Irish, but also it was hoped that the United States would soon join the war against Germany.

The rebellion now had its martyrs, and their deaths and the thousands of arrests and hundreds of casualties, often involving innocent people, hardened opinions about Ireland again. Although negotiations between Redmond for the South, Carson for Ulster and Lloyd George for the British Government nearly achieved immediate Home Rule for the south with Ulster remaining in the Union, Unionist politicians at Westminster squashed any real hope of this becoming law. Moreover the nationalist Irishmen became convinced, too late in one sense, that force was the only weapon that would succeed, and the martyrs of the Easter Rising had been right after all. In subsequent bye-elections, the Sinn Fein candidates were voted into power at the expense of Redmond's Irish Nationalist party, and in 1918, in the "Coupon Election" at the end of the war, only 6 Irish Nationalists were elected in the constituencies outside Ulster. The other seventy-three seats were all captured by the Sinn Feiners including Countess Markievicz, the first woman candidate elected to Parliament, but they all refused to come to Westminster, setting themselves up instead as an Irish Parliament or Dail in Dublin. (In practice thirty-six of those elected could not come to London; they were in gaol.)

Sinn Fein now set about destroying English control in Ireland. Griffith, Collins and De Valera organised terrorists and caused trouble in any way they could. The British retaliated in 1920 by setting up a new type of police force, recruited from English volunteer ex-soldiers, who became known from their khaki uniforms and black belts as the "Black and Tans". They and the Royal Irish Constabulary met force with force, terror with terror. Casualties on both sides mounted, totalling perhaps 1,500 killed and an enormous but unknown number injured. A state of war prevailed when Lloyd George at length got Parliament to pass the "Government of Ireland Act" in December 1920, which divided Ireland into two parts (six counties of Ulster, and the rest), and gave them both Home Rule as well as continued representation at Westminster. Ulster accepted the Act; the South did not and the "Irish Republican Army" fought on. Only after George V had risked assassination and gone personally to open the first Northern Ireland Parliament in Belfast in June 1921, there to speak passionately of the need to end civil war, was a cease-fire

75

arranged in July, which in December 1921 was transformed into a complicated peace treaty approved by the Westminster Parliament.

It was narrowly approved by the Dail in 1922, and the Irish Free State came into legitimate existence, being the whole of Ireland without Ulster. The "Black and Tans" were disbanded; the last British troops left Ireland in December 1922, leaving the Sinn Fein movement and its military wing, the I.R.A., to fight their own civil war as to whether or not the treaty should be accepted. The pro-treaty men won by April 1923, and it was thereafter widely accepted that the Irish Free State had become a self-governing member of the British Commonwealth, with the same status as, for example, Canada. Britain retained naval rights in three Irish ports, and appointed a Governor-General, a man of very little power or influence. In all other respects, Home Rule was achieved.

The battle was ended. The Irish Free State, later to call itself Eire and to leave the Commonwealth, had its independence; Ulster, or Northern Ireland, was both linked to Great Britain within the Union and yet also had a greater measure of self-determination on internal matters. But laws and treaties do not change attitudes overnight; Protestants in the North still despised the Catholics there, and frequently discriminated against them, while in the South, the "All-Ireland" men kept alive in the I.R.A. and in certain branches of Sinn Fein the ambition that one day the whole island would be freed from any British connection, and that total control would pass to the representatives of the native Irish Catholics.

Thus, more than half a century later, Sisyphus is still at work.

CHAPTER SIX

A Really New World? 1918–1929

The Great War was over, and the peacemakers were at Versailles endeavouring to ensure that there could never be another catastrophe like it. The women over thirty had won the vote, and established once and for all the principle of female suffrage. In Ireland, the "time of troubles" persisted, but slowly the fuse was to burn itself out, allowing the cease-fire of July 1921. It must have seemed as if reality could be brought to a speech by Lloyd George made in 1917: "Don't always be thinking of getting back to where you were before the war; get a really new world." In the eighteen months after the Armistice in November 1918, four million men took off their uniforms for the last time, and came home to see the results of what they had fought for.

Visible changes were easily picked out. The pre-war woman had been a creature of curves and coyness, of long hair and long skirts. Now she was an independent and challenging being, with not just an ankle peeping out from beneath her skirt, but often a dress so short that her knees were visible. She was no longer a helpless prisoner in the home, but often a skilled and experienced worker. Unasked she voiced her opinions about anything, and she smoked cigarettes through an absurdly long holder. Men's dress too had changed; the Edwardian frock-coat and top hat had almost entirely disappeared, to be replaced by the "lounge suit", leaving the tailcoat to be used only on the most formal occasions like weddings. Even after the war, there was rationing of food in one way or another until the Ministry of Food was abolished in 1921. Despite the complaints of the farmers who said it upset their cows, there was an Act of Parliament which made everyone set their clocks one hour earlier in the summertime, in order to save valuable fuel by making better use of the daylight. Renewed annually from 1916 to 1925, this was made permanent in the latter year, and the phrase "British Summer Time" was introduced. Where pastimes were concerned, the cinema was the newest form of entertainment; "moving pictures" had been heard of before the war, but now they were becoming commonplace, and so too was a new type of rhythmic music,

Not all was drab and wretched in the middle of the 1920s,
as this exotic London cabaret scene indicates.

known first as "ragtime" and later coming under the general heading of "jazz".

Attitudes were changed too. In 1914 men had volunteered for war service and were hailed as heroes. In 1915 women had stuck white feathers denoting cowardice into the lapels of men who they felt were young enough or fit enough to join the volunteers. In 1916 all males between the ages of 18 and 41 (later 51) became legally liable to be called up as a matter of patriotic duty. And for what? The survivors were home again, and yet those who had remained at home did not seem to understand what they had been through, and the soldiers themselves began to question why they had been through it and why they had left three quarters of a million fellows dead overseas. It was all very well to hear Lloyd George calling for "homes fit for heroes to live in", but there was little comfort in words. In short, there was to be a brief period of rejoicing and relief after the war, but when that was over, the main work of reconstruction had to be done, for the changes that had occurred were largely glossy and unreal, and the basic problems of the British economic and political system had still to be faced. The war had accelerated things rather than altered them, for most of what happened in the twenties had its roots in the pre-war world.

A miner's wife going to the pawn shop during a coal strike in 1921.

The most striking example of this acceleration occurs in the field of politics. The presence of men like John Burns in the same party as Herbert Asquith illustrates the difficulty of the nineteenth-century Liberal Party trying to encompass the twentieth-century electorate. We have already seen how the Labour Representation Committee was set up in 1900, winning two Parliamentary seats in that year under the guidance of its secretary James Ramsay MacDonald. This new party, representing the working man and the ideas of socialism and trade unionism, was helped into existence by a decision of the House of Lords in 1901 that the Amalgated Society of Railway Servants was responsible for a strike on the Taff Vale Railway in South Wales, and owed the railway line managers £42,000 for its costs and damages. This decision was so biased against the whole idea of Trade Unions and the strike weapon that the L.R.C. decided to step up its pressure to get men into Parliament. Three more were elected between 1901 and 1903 in by-elections, the last one, Arthur Henderson, defeating candidates of both the major parties. In 1906, "Labour" representation in the Commons grew to 53, of whom 29 were officially sponsored by the L.R.C., and the movement was officially renamed the Labour Party.

The two elections of 1910 were strongly focused on the issues

79

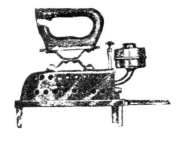

At the beginning of our period, most 'middle class' homes could boast of at least one servant—a maid, a cook, a nanny or perhaps a governess. As money became scarce, these human helps were enticed or partly replaced by mechanical aids, but even by the end of the period such gadgets were relatively primitive, and most of these examples, taken from the catalogue of the much respected 'Army and Navy Stores' of 1937–38, would not have seemed out of place in the catalogue of the Great Exhibition at Crystal Palace in 1851. They indicate that although electric or gas lighting was commonplace, these power sources were not yet in widespread use for refrigerators, irons, washing machines, sewing machines or cooking.

Refrigerators were insulated boxes into which the owner put chunks of ice bought from a shop.

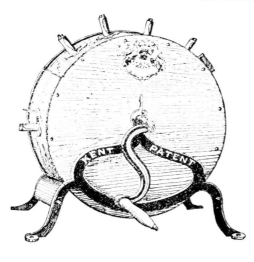

Washing clothes was a laborious business, involving pumping a handle to swirl the clothes round in a drum followed by winding them through a wringer to get out the surplus water (at much cost to buttons). Cooking could be done on gas or electric stoves, but oil was also used, and so were solid fuel burners, the latter providing one example which is not unfamiliar in the last quarter of the twentieth century.

Unless a household had such a stove or some fairly elaborate kitchen range, hot running water was unusual. Some houses had self-lighting gas boilers over the bath, but there were no immersion heaters, no central heating units and no air conditioning. Electricity was not yet applied to mixers, nor to sewing machines. Keeping a family clean, tidy and well-fed required considerable physical effort by our standards.

of the People's Budget and the powers of the House of Lords, and
the voters concentrated on the two major parties. The Labour
party won 40 and 42 seats, in each case collecting about 7% of the
total number of votes cast. But in the "Coupon" election of 1918,
Labour won 22% of the votes, and with 63 seats in the Commons
became the second largest party, if we discount the 73 Sinn Fein
members who refused to take up their seats, and therefore the
official opposition to the government of Lloyd George. Ramsay
MacDonald, Arthur Henderson and Philip Snowden, the three
most talented Labour leaders, failed to get elected in their chosen
constituencies, however, and the Parliamentary party fell into
disarray. However the other parties were having their difficulties
too. The Liberals, who had been elected overwhelmingly in 1906
under Sir Henry Campbell-Bannerman, and who under Asquith
from 1908 to 1916 had clung to power in the 1910 elections and
passed a number of highly important pieces of social legislation,
were breaking up. Stuck in the middle between the tradition-
alism of the Conservatives and the new ideas of the Labour party,
they lost supporters to both sides, and became uncertain of what
they stood for. Asquith's favourite answer to a difficult problem
was "Wait and see", and it won him few friends. By 1916, he
had lost the respect of the House of Commons and of many of his
own party, and his place at the head of the wartime Coalition
government (which he had introduced in 1915) was taken by the
"Welsh Wizard", Lloyd George. They were totally different
types of man, and personality clashes were to help to shape the
new political future. When the war was won in 1918, success
could not be claimed by any party, since the government had
been one of all parties. Lloyd George was hailed as "the man who
won the war", and he intended to reap the harvest of his
popularity. But he had insufficient Liberal support, which was
divided between him and his type of politics and Asquith and his
type, and he needed continued Conservative support as he had
enjoyed in the years of coalition.

The Conservatives, similarly, knew that they had not done

Lloyd George electioneering in his native Wales.

anything distinctive enough to win the support of the electorate in the past thirteen years; the last time they had been in power was when they had split up over the issue of Free Trade in 1905. They needed the magic of their association with Lloyd George if they were to hold onto power in any form. Thus they agreed to a scheme which Lloyd George produced for the 1918 election. The Lloyd George government would bid to stay in power not on party policies, but on whether or not the electors would favour Lloyd George and his supporters. These supporters, whether they were nominally Liberals or Conservatives, received a letter of recommendation which they could show to their voters, signed by Lloyd George and by Bonar Law, the Conservative leader. Disparagingly referred to by Asquith as "the Coupon", (a new word brought back from France and denoting rationing and scarcity), this letter gave its name to the whole campaign, and brought massive triumph to Lloyd George. His Coupon coalition won 478 seats out of the total of 707, though significantly 339 of his supporters were Coalition Unionists (Conservatives), and there were a further 48 non-Coupon Conservatives in the House. The non-Coupon Liberals' defeat was such that even Asquith failed to get returned, in a seat which he had previously held for 32 years.

Lloyd George's government could only last as long as his personal magnetism held parties and people together. Having

83

"won the war", he now had to make sense of the peace. His government had already passed an Education Act in 1918 which gave full time schooling to all children up to the age of 14. In 1919 it went on to produce a Coal Mines Act which gave a seven-hour working day to the miners and continued government subsidies to the mine-owners, and a Housing Act which set out to produce, under local council control, as many as possible of the 800,000 new houses which were required. In 1920 a new Unemployment Insurance Act was added to the list, which was extended in 1921 so that the State was being made responsible for the poor and unemployed, instead of the local authorities. These were broadly popular but slow-acting measures, but Lloyd George's image did not remain untarnished for long.

Always a complicated and devious man, he attracted enemies and failed to keep friends. His Irish "solution" lost him some supporters; the fact that British troops were nearly involved in war in Turkey in 1922 lost him some more, perhaps unfairly. Dissatisfaction with the workings of the Versailles peace treaties came to the fore, and in 1922 the "Honours Scandal" broke, when it became apparent that those who gave money or support to Lloyd George's political cause were being rewarded with peerages and knighthoods. In October 1922, the Conservatives felt that they no longer needed to shelter behind the increasingly discredited figure of the former hero, and they announced the end of the Coalition. Lloyd George resigned. Bonar Law was asked to form a government, and party politics started again after a seven year pause. In the subsequent election, the Conservatives won 345 seats and the Labour party 142. Lloyd George's Liberals had 62, and Asquith's Liberals ("Squiffites") 54. It was a secure majority, but Law's government did little before he resigned with cancer of the throat in May 1923. Many, including Lord Curzon himself, expected Lord Curzon to be appointed the new Prime Minister, for he was an experienced and highly skilled politician and administrator. But he was a Lord, and the official Opposition, the Labour Party, had hardly any support in the Lords, and

Stanley Baldwin in 1922. He led a brief ministry in 1923, and was Prime Minister from 1924 to 1929, a period dominated by the General Strike of 1926.

therefore it would have been impossible for them to exercise their right to question the leader of the Government. Curzon was passed over in favour of an almost unknown businessman, who had only recently been Law's Chancellor of the Exchequer, Stanley Baldwin.

Stanley Baldwin had two gifts which the Commons respected after the years of Lloyd George's flamboyance and rhetoric: he spoke and acted with quiet, unpushing sincerity, and as a result of his business upbringing, he was very aware of the financial problems of the country, and the growing spectre of unemployment. He decided to reactivate the bomb which had blown the Conservatives apart in the first few years of the century, the explosive issue of Free Trade or Protection and Imperial Preference. But as this had not been a part of the Conservatives' election plans in 1922, he felt obliged to call another election, despite the contrary advice of all whom he consulted. The result was disastrous for Baldwin and his party. In the 1923 election, the Conservatives won 258 seats, the Labour party 191 and the Liberals, reunited as committed Free Traders, 159. No party held an overall majority, and Baldwin did not resign until his government was defeated on a vote of "No Confidence" in January 1924. It seemed likely that the Labour and Liberal parties

Left to right: Macdonald the starveling clerk, Thomas the engine-driver, Henderson the foundry-labourer and Clynes the mill-hand leaving Buckingham Palace after a Privy Council Meeting in January 1924.

could work together as a government, and so George V sent for the leader of the larger party, Ramsay MacDonald, to ask if he could form a ministry.

"Today 23 years ago" wrote the King in his diary "dear Grandmama died. I wonder what she would have thought of a Labour Government." What indeed? Political change had accelerated so much since 1901 that even the Labour members were mentally breathless. As J. R. Clynes recalled: "As we stood waiting for His Majesty amid the gold and crimson magnificence of the Palace, I could not help marvelling at the strange turn of Fortune's wheel which had brought Ramsay MacDonald the starveling clerk, Thomas the engine-driver, Henderson the foundry-labourer, and Clynes the mill-hand, to this pinnacle beside the man whose forebears had been kings for so many splendid generations." The first moral problem that the Labour Ministers had to face was whether or not they would agree to wear court dress, which seemed too aristocratic for their background. MacDonald insisted, and court dress was worn.

No government passes many bills in its first few months, and the Labour Government was no exception. It produced a respectable "Free Traders" budget, passed a new Housing Act, and increased and guaranteed unemployment benefits. Its foreign policy was more spectacular, but achieved little before a strange incident brought the government down. In the autumn of

SAFETY FIRST

Mr. Ramsay MacDonald has been fully equal to the heavy responsibilities of Prime Minister.

He has filled the great position with entire adequacy at a time of exceptional difficulty.

The settlement with France is a brilliant feather in his cap.

To have succeeded where Bonar Law, Baldwin and Lloyd George failed is a considerable achievement.

—The Daily News LIBERAL NEWSPAPER

The LABOUR PARTY
WORKS for PEACE

In the 1924 Election, the Labour Party made much of its foreign policy successes, as this poster shows. The slogan 'Safety First' did not save them from defeat after the campaign had been knocked sideways by the 'Zinoviev letter'; 'Safety First' was also adopted by Baldwin as his motto in 1929, and he too was defeated.

1924, a Communist magazine, *The Workers' Weekly*, published an article calling on soldiers not to shoot down working class comrades in military or industrial disputes. With the memory of the Russian Revolutions of 1917 ringing in all heads, two opinions were possible. Such a statement was either treason, or it was a fair exercise of free speech. The Director of Public Prosecutions decided that the editor of the magazine, Campbell, should be sent for trial. The Labour Attorney-General withdrew the prosecution. MacDonald found the House of Commons seriously split, and asked the King to dissolve Parliament so that the country could decide whether they wanted a Labour Government or not.

The third General Election in three years produced a strange result after an even stranger campaign. Four days before people were due to vote, the Foreign Office sent to *The Times* a copy of a letter which seemed to come from Zinoviev, then the head of the Russian-based Communist International movement. The letter said that the Labour government of Britain was too middle-class, and that all true Communists in Britain should try to infiltrate not only the Trade Unions but also the armed forces. There are many unanswered questions about the incident. Was the letter a fake? Why did the Foreign Office publish it? How much difference did it really make to the election result?

When the votes were counted, the Conservatives had an

overwhelming 419 seats, to Labour's 151 and the Liberals' 40. At first sight, the Labour Party appears to have been savagely rejected by the people, but in fact they received over a million more votes than they had in the 1923 election which had left them in power. The real victims of the Zinoviev letter were the Liberals, who lost nearly $1\frac{1}{2}$ million votes. With possible revolution just round the corner, it was not a time for voters to stand in the centre of the political road. More chose to seek shelter on the Conservative side than on the Labour, and Stanley Baldwin was thus swept back into power with a record majority. There he remained for the full term of office, the first man to do so since the five year rule had been introduced in the Parliament Act of 1911, and that despite all the economic troubles which had their peak in the General Strike of 1926.

The Great War had accelerated and accentuated Britain's economic problems. It was ludicrous to expect "Great" Britain, with only 0.2% of the land area of the world, to remain great once the industrial giants of America and Germany had started to develop at speed. Even before the War, pressure had been growing on all the basic nineteenth-century industries which had made Britain the industrial leader of the world—coalmining, shipbuilding, steel-production and textiles work. The Trade Unions had tried to protect the interests of their members, but what they were really fighting was not, as they seemed to think, the employers but the cold, hard facts of international economic competition. Strikes were common in the years just before the war, among cotton-workers, miners, boilermakers, railwaymen, dockers, seamen and even firemen, and an ominous sign appeared when in 1913 the new National Union of Railwaymen formed a "Triple Alliance" with the Transport Workers' Federation (which included most dockers) and the Miners' Federation. Such an army of workers could obviously bring the country to a halt if they all went on strike at the same time, and indeed, that threat was the intention and the strength of the Alliance.

An agitator addresses a group of workers; Wigan, 1921.

After the war, the economy prospered as businesses started up again and people bought all those things of which the war had deprived them. But by the middle of 1920, the situation was worsening rapidly. Foreign competition was depressing the English market, and firm after firm closed down as it was unable to sell its goods. More and more men joined the queue of unemployed, shuffling forward to collect the benefits which the Government had promised but which it never expected to have to pay on such a vast scale. In 1921, two million people were registered as unemployed, and the total never fell below one million (or roughly 10% of the registered work force) until 1936; the average for the 1920s was 12%.

In no industry was the strain greater than in coal-mining, where foreign competition combined with the growing use of oil and petrol greatly reduced the demand for British coal. Moreover the seams that the men were picking out were nearly exhausted and often far from the main pit shaft, making the work more dangerous and frustrating than it had ever been, and less profitable. The Sankey Commission, whose report had led to the Coal Mines Act of 1919, with shorter working days and government subsidies for the owners, did not manage to save the pits from falling production, increasing inefficiency and dismissals. The King does not have any right to act on matters of political and economic significance unless asked to do so by the Prime Minister, but George V felt compelled to write to his Prime Minister in 1921 "His Majesty does most earnestly trust that the Government will agree to some scheme by which work, and not doles (benefit payments) will be supplied to the unemployed, the great majority of whom honestly want to work." He was right, but unemployment continued, and was perhaps made worse by "The Geddes Axe" in 1922, when in order to save money the Government cut back on its own spending on health, education and the armed services.

By 1925 the Government felt it could no longer afford to subsidise the mines. The mine-owners retorted that either the men must go back to working eight hours at the face each shift, or their wages must be reduced. The miners threatened to strike: "not a minute on the day, not a penny off the pay" became their slogan. The Government appointed the Samuel Commission to investigate the mining industry, and after six strenuous months,

A pit pony being brought up to the daylight before a strike; Wigan, 1921.

its report was published in March 1926. It wanted better working conditions and family allowances for the men, the amalgamation of smaller pits into more efficient units, the nationalization of coal royalties; but, in the short run, it could see no way of avoiding cuts in wages. The miners exploded in furious despair. April 1926 was spent in hours of deadlocked argument with employers and government, but the fact remained that from May 1st, the miners were to work for reduced wages. On that day, therefore, the implicit threat of the Triple Alliance was called into being; Trade Unionism played its Ace of Trumps, and called a General Strike, to start on May 3rd.

Most strikers had nothing to gain from it. It was not their quarrel and it did not involve their wages or their conditions. The only people who might benefit from it were the miners. Similarly, most middle class men were not personally involved though they were bound to be inconvenienced as miners, transport workers, builders, gas and electricity men all stopped work. The General

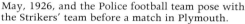

May, 1926, and the Police football team pose with the Strikers' team before a match in Plymouth.

Strike was therefore remarkably free from personal bitterness, except in a few areas. Policemen watching over strikers soon found themselves playing football against them. Troops were used only at London Docks for the preservation of order, and once to escort one hundred empty lorries from Hyde Park to the docks in order to load flour and meat from the ships there. Undergraduates, middle class and aristocratic volunteers, ex-Army and Navy officers came forward to drive lorries, buses and trains, and much of the spirit of the strike is summed up by a story told by Sir Philip Gibbs, who wanted to get to Manchester. ''I decided to try my luck, and went to Euston early one morning . . . After a long wait a cheery young gentleman advanced along the platform and raised a bowler hat. 'Good morning everybody', he said. 'I'm the engine driver; I hope to get you as far

Troops in Hyde Park prepare to escort food from London Docks, May 1926.

as Manchester . . .' He put on a pair of white gloves and smiled at the small crowd. 'Very nice of you to come,' he said. 'It shows great faith in me.' '' He got them nearly as far as Harrow, and then the train came off the rails. ''Our gentleman driver alighted and raised his bowler hat again with a cheery smile. 'That's torn it,' he said. 'So sorry. Some little thing went wrong.' ''

George V was very conscious of the spirit which prevailed during the Strike. As he wrote in his diary, ''Our old country can well be proud of itself, as during the last nine days there has been a strike in which 4 million men have been affected; not a shot has been fired and no one killed; it shows what a wonderful people we are . . .'' His facts were broadly true, though three thousand people were prosecuted later for violence or incitement. But there had been remarkably little tension; the newspapers either failed

The food convoy passes through the East End, led by an armoured car.

Left: A London Tram with volunteer drivers. *Right:* A volunteer driver cranks the engine of his London bus during the General Strike. Note the protection for both driver and engine.

to come out at all or in such small degrees that they could whip up no passions. Sir John Reith kept the B.B.C. strictly neutral, to the indignation of Winston Churchill, who instead produced a rather bad Government newspaper called the *British Gazette*. The Government did little else except indicate its willingness to discuss things, and the Triple Alliance had no obvious leaders who could speak for all the striking workers. On May 12th the Strike collapsed, and no one had gained anything, least of all the miners, who steadfastly remained on strike until the scourge of near-starvation sent them back down the pits in November, to hew out the coal in return for longer hours and lower wages.

Trade Unionism had suffered a severe blow. To use one's strongest weapon and to find that it is totally ineffective is to fail disastrously and publicly. Membership dropped, and workers got down to making the best of a bad situation as well as they could. Baldwin's government maintained stability for the next three years, and apart from the miners, everyone was better off in 1929 than they had been in 1926.

It was with considerable confidence that Baldwin and the Conservatives entered the 1929 election with the slogan "Safety First". They had brought the country through its most testing time since the War, and in 1928 they had given the vote to several million "flappers" (women aged 21–30), who had every reason therefore to be kindly disposed towards them. But when the results were announced early in June 1929, the Labour party had won 288 seats, the Conservatives 260 and the Liberals 59. Baldwin resigned at once, and Ramsay MacDonald became Prime Minister again, dependent as before on the support of the Liberals if he was to govern effectively. This he might have done but for the fact that on October 24th, less than five months after his election, confidence collapsed on the American Stock Exchange in Wall Street, New York, and the western world was thrown into a financial whirlpool more turbulent and more destructive than could be imagined at first. It not only sucked down the Labour government of Ramsay MacDonald and thus affected British domestic politics in the Thirties; it also spewed up strength into the arms of the extremists like Hitler and Mussolini, whose attitudes were to colour British and world history blood-red before the decade was out.

Small Boy (proudly). "MY DADDY WAS A SPECIAL CONSTABLE IN THE STRIKE."
Small Girl (still more proudly). "MY DADDY WAS A STOKER ON A REAL LIVE ENGINE, AND MUMMY SAYS HE'S NOT CLEAN YET."

'Punch's' view of the middle class attitude to the Strike.

'Wouldn't it be marvellous, Mr Shaw' cooed the flapper 'if we were to
marry? Our children could have your brains and my beauty.' 'Have you
considered, madam' said the writer heavily 'the possibility that they
might be blessed the other way round?'

The flapper was a creature of exaggerated enthusiasms, as the word
'flapper' disparagingly indicated. It referred to girls in their late teens and
to young women in the nineteen twenties who were enjoying a freedom
which no generation of women had had before. Many of the old male
barriers were breaking down in economic and social life; there were many
new job opportunities of all sorts, and the idea of women having their
own respectable career was accepted at last. Only the Stock Exchange and
the Church of England remained firmly opposed to accepting women in
responsible positions, and women challenged male supremacy in
numerous ways. They were considerably liberated by the changes in

styles of dress. What had started as an economy measure in the war became a focal point of fashion; hemlines moved up until they were well above the knee, allowing the flapper to dance with abandon, to ride motor-cycles (pillions were briefly known as 'flapper-brackets'), to play more sport ('Anyone for tennis?' became a catch-word) and altogether to move more quickly. The boyishness of the flapper was also emphasised by her attempt to appear flat-chested and to wear her hair short. She smoked and spoke out more in public, travelled and went to social events without a chaperon, and above all she *enjoyed* her life-style. She was an exuberant, positive person, looked upon by many of the older generation as being irresponsible, by herself as irrepressible. In 1928 the 'flapper' was given the vote on the same terms as men (i.e., all over 21), and that victory together with the Depression in the 1930s curbed the excesses of the young women and made them respectable once again.

CHAPTER SEVEN

Years of Fear 1929–1936

The ticker-tapes spilled across the floor of the Wall Street Stock Exchange, but the dealers were no longer looking at them. They knew that all the complicated statistics held but one message: "sell, sell, sell". As they stood numbly exhausted by the day's official trading they were well aware that an unprecedented catastrophe had occurred, the price of which was bound to be much more than the cost in personal fortunes. Men who buy and sell stocks and shares understand the risks and allow for them in their dealings, but when prices collapsed so devastatingly in October 1929, the damage was suffered by millions of men and women in the western world, many of whom did not even know what stocks and shares were, let alone own any.

Most businesses are built up on borrowed money, which is got by selling certificates which entitle the purchaser to a "share" in the ownership and profits of the company. Most "share-holders" are content to allow the directors to run the company, provided that they receive their regular payment of a "dividend", a dividing-up of the profits in proportion to the number of shares that each man holds. If a shareholder is unhappy about the amount of profit that he receives, he can sell his shares on a "Stock Exchange", for the best price that he can get, which might be more than he originally paid, or it might be less. If business is bad and profits are low, then almost certainly a shareholder will only be able to turn his shares back into cash by asking a very small price for them. Confidence is the important key to good prices on the Stock Exchange, and in 1929, confidence in America suddenly evaporated. Men who had thought themselves rich because of their holdings of shares found that they were paupers. Several of the "richest" men in America committed suicide when they realised that their wealth was scarcely worth the paper on which it was printed. Anyone who had lent money now demanded it back, in hard cash and not in promises to pay, and no one could afford to sell anything on credit, for they needed the cash to pay for raw materials and wages. Thus the economies of Britain, France and Germany were at once put under extra strain,

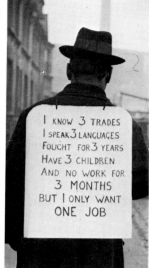

Work on a production line in the Morris car factory at Cowley, Oxford, in 1930.
Factory work was repetitive and dull . . . but better than no work at all.

for they were inextricably bound up with American businesses
and banks, and a vicious circle developed. Without cash,
companies collapsed, and were unable to pay their debts or
employ their workers. Without pay in their pockets, workers
were unable to buy much from the shops and so other companies
found themselves without cash coming in.

In 1929, just over one million men and women were
unemployed in Britain. As the vicious circle spun round, this
figure went up to two and a half million by the end of 1930. An
unkind fate had decreed that the Labour Party, which
represented the ordinary working man, should be in power with
Liberal support just at the moment when the lot of the working
man was getting worse and worse, and the Labour Party had no
positive answer to the crisis. As the Depression deepened, only
one man from the Labour benches in Parliament had any strong
ideas about remedies for the situation, and he was an ex-
Conservative M.P., Oswald Mosley. The Government rejected his
theories, and left him to form his own "New Party", which soon
became the basis of Fascism in Britain, with strong similarities of
attitude to that of Mussolini in Italy, and later, Hitler in Germany.

For Ramsay MacDonald, who was already being accused by
some of the Labour Party of preferring the company of aristocrats
to that of men of his own background, there seemed no solution
that could reduce the hardships of the country. It was believed

99

Oswald Mosley, flanked by Landseer's lions at the foot of Nelson's column and protected by his black-shirted guards, harangues a crowd. The New Party shows its Fascist tendencies, 1932.

by all economists that the Government *must* "balance the Budget" (spend no more than it received in taxation), and this was a policy that had been used in 1922 on the recommendation of Sir Eric Geddes. His "Axe" had cut spending on education, health and welfare as well as on the Civil Service and the armed forces, and although there was no proof that it had done any good then, it was still the accepted medicine for economic ailments. In the short run, it was bound to mean more jobless, and less benefits. The other touchstone of economic policy was that Britain should be "on the Gold Standard", which meant that anyone could exchange their paper pound note for gold at the banks. This had been suspended during the war, but in 1925 Winston Churchill, who later described himself as "the worst Chancellor of the Exchequer of the century" put the country back on the Standard. It was another gamble on continuing confidence, and it worked for a while, but it made British exports more expensive, and that meant that less was sold abroad, and that in turn also meant more unemployment.

By 1931, the situation was desperate. The Wall Street crash had made Americans call back money that they had lent, and very reluctant to lend any more, and by July 1931 Britain urgently needed to borrow gold. Because the country was on the Gold Standard, any foreigners who had any pounds were changing paper back into metal, and the reserves of bullion were running very low. To make matters worse, a committee led by Sir George May calculated that to balance the Budget would require a

The classic pose of the unemployed in the 1930s.

further cut in unemployment benefits, amounting to over £66,000,000, and heavy taxation. This Report was a knife in the heart of the Labour party. National and international confidence bled away as fast as the remaining gold in the Bank of England's vaults, and it was clear that only the full acceptance of the Report could save the country. The Cabinet met, argued, and split; eleven of its members were prepared, reluctantly but in the national interest, to make all the necessary economies, but nine men, most of whom spoke for the Trade Unionist members of the Party, preferred to resign. Late in the evening, Ramsay MacDonald, looking very angry and hurt, stormed out of the meeting. "I am off to the Palace," he shouted, "to throw in my hand."

The English monarch is like a safety valve on a complicated machine. One hopes that it will never be called into operation, but when it is, it must save the machine from destroying itself. To George V therefore came the task of maintaining a government, and saving the country from total financial chaos. His choice of a new Prime Minister was all-important. He might have chosen the Liberal Lloyd George, who had saved the country in an emergency once before, but he had just had a major operation. He might have chosen the Conservative Stanley Baldwin, hurriedly recalled from his holiday in France, but the last General Election had rejected him, and there was no time to have another one to see if the country would give a different verdict. His own preference was the man who had just "thrown in his hand",

101

COUNTRY FIRST!

NATIONAL PARTY

VOTE!

A drawing in 'Punch' encourages support for MacDonald's National Government.

Ramsay MacDonald, who could lead a National Government of Cooperation which would restore everyone's confidence. The Liberal and Conservative leaders were prepared to back him while the crisis continued, and so that was what George V arranged. In August 1931, a National Government was formed which had the support of all but one of the Liberals in Parliament, and of all of the Conservatives—but, by contrast, only twelve members of the Labour Party would support their own party leader in his new situation.

MacDonald went ahead with what had to be done, although he was branded as a traitor to the working classes, and was expelled from the party which he had helped to raise from its insignificant early days to its ruling position in 1924 and 1929. Early in September his Chancellor of the Exchequer, Philip Snowden, one of the few Labour ministers to stay loyal to him, passed an emergency Budget, which cut by 10% the money paid by the state to a whole range of people, from Cabinet ministers at the top, to members of the armed services in the middle, and to the unemployed at the bottom. Teachers' pay was cut by 15%; that of policemen by 5%. Parliament accepted the Budget, even though the majority of the Labour members voted against it.

It seemed to do the trick. American and French bankers immediately lent the country £80,000,000, and confidence began to grow again, but on September 15th came incredible news. The 12,000 sailors of the Royal Navy ships in harbour at Invergordon learned of their cuts in pay when they read their newspapers, and

The *Daily Mirror* tells
of the Invergordon Mutiny.

THE DAILY MIRROR, Wednesday, Sept. 16, 1931.

NAVAL SENSATION—PAGE 3

Daily Mirror

THE DAILY PICTURE   NEWSPAPER WITH THE LARGEST NET SALE

No. 8,680 | Registered at the G.P.O. as a Newspaper. WEDNESDAY, SEPTEMBER 16, 1931 | One Penny | *Full Wireless on Page 14*

UNREST IN THE NAVY: EXERCISES SUSPENDED FOR PAY CUTS INVESTIGATION

Rear-Admiral Wilfred Tomkinson, who was posted Rear-Admiral Commanding Battle-Cruiser Squadron last April.

A painting party in the Atlantic Fleet battleship Rodney.

The battle-cruiser Hood, in which Rear-Admiral Tomkinson is flying his flag.

H.M.S. Nelson. She and the Rodney have a crew of 1,314 when carrying full complement.

Destroyers of the Atlantic Fleet passing the Forth Bridge on their way to commence the manoeuvres which have been suspended.

According to a statement issued yesterday by the Admiralty, the senior officer of the Atlantic Fleet, Rear-Admiral Wilfred Tomkinson, has reported that the promulgation of the reduced rates in naval pay has led to unrest amongst a proportion of the lower ratings. In consequence he has deemed it desirable to suspend the Fleet exercises while representations of the hardships occasioned by certain of the cuts are investigated in order that they may be reported for consideration by the Board of the Admiralty.

they refused to go on parade. The autumn naval manoeuvres were cancelled, and the Admiralty board met hurriedly, and pressed the government to reduce the cuts. The "Mutiny" was soon over, but it had done enormous damage to that thin trickle of confidence. On September 16th, £5,000,000 in gold was withdrawn from the Bank of England; on September 17th, £10,000,000; on September 19th, £18,000,000. The precious £80,000,000 was evaporating so fast that new emergency measures had to be taken at once. On September 21st the Government announced a reduction in most of the pay cuts, and at last took Britain off the Gold Standard. The value of the pound immediately fell, but otherwise, nothing drastic happened. The Invergordon Mutiny had achieved what the Government had been trying to do, namely put an end to the financial chaos. Because the pound was less expensive, Britain's exports became cheaper, and so the amount sold abroad went up. The worst moment of the crisis was over, and in the breathing space, a new General Election could be called.

The result was an overwhelming victory for the National Government under Ramsay MacDonald, with 521 seats, mostly Conservative. The Labour Party was reduced to a mere 52, the Liberals to 33; the Communists and Mosley's New Party had no success whatsoever. It was another record majority, and it kept MacDonald in power until he handed over to the leader of the Conservatives, Stanley Baldwin, in 1935. MacDonald had assumed office believing that the crisis would soon be over, and that he might be able to resume his place in the Labour Party before too much damage had been done to the unity of the movement, but that was not to be. Instead, bitterness increased for three reasons, and further reduced the little support that he had received from some members of the party.

In the first place, the Conservative majority in the National Government now believed in tariffs and Protection, which Philip Snowden could not support. He was therefore "promoted" to the House of Lords, and in 1932 the new Chancellor of the

Exchequer, Neville Chamberlain, at last introduced a general tariff of 10% on all imports, the very measure which his father had had in mind when he split the Conservatives in the early years of the century. Joseph Chamberlain's widow was in the Public Gallery of the House of Commons to hear her husband's ideas being made law. The Labour Party fought against the act, without success.

Secondly, the 1931 Government introduced the idea of the "means test", whereby those who were unemployed had to answer questions about their savings and the incomes of other members of the family before they received their full benefit from the state. Not only did this appear to be prying into people's private lives; it also penalised the man who had managed to set some money aside, and split up families when the presence of one wage-earner in the group meant that the benefit for the others was reduced.

But the third and most pressing reason for the Labour Party's dissatisfaction with the National Government was that unemployment continued on a massive scale. It reached its peak in the winter of 1932-3, when there were more than 3,000,000 men and women out of work, some of whom had given up registering themselves as such because they saw no point in joining the weekly queues at the Labour Exchanges. Some areas were worse hit than others; those where shipbuilding or steelmaking or mining was the major industry often became places without hope, even though some of them received new factories and works financed by the Government. None was better known than Jarrow, the steelmaking and shipbuilding town which became known as "the town that was murdered" when two-thirds of its workforce was on the dole.

As the economy of the country slowly recovered in the middle years of the 1930s, it was just 200 men from Jarrow who started out on a three hundred mile march to London, to remind the Government of 1936 that Tyneside was still suffering the humiliation and the problems of 1929. "March" is the wrong

105

The Jarrow Marchers near Bedford; October 1936.

word; they called it the "Jarrow Crusade", but that conjures up a false picture too: it was a walk, a shuffle for some, that could have no immediate reward for those taking part except the feeling that they had done something to drive away the soul-destroying boredom and bitterness that grew out of being unwillingly idle for so long. Badly fed and often inadequately clothed for the journey, they pressed southwards, sometimes greeted by brass bands and sympathetic crowds, sometimes filing through streets of embarrassed onlookers with no sound except the clatter of their own boots and the toneless notes of a few reedy mouth-organs which they carried. They slept in village halls, in school classrooms; they gulped the food and drink that was offered to them by well-wishers. Their ranks swelled and swelled by thousands until they spilled into London.

Their target was achieved, and yet what was that achievement? It was one of the spirit only. No new employers rushed to Jarrow, though in 1937 the Government did provide money for an industrial estate at Gateshead, further up the Tyne, which at the most gave jobs to about 4,000 men.

It was not the Jarrow March of 1936 that brought an end to unemployment, but the marching of different types of armies. In 1936 Italian troops marched into Abyssinia; German troops marched into the Rhineland; in Spain senior officers led by General Franco marched on Madrid against the elected Govern-

Rearmament helped reduce unemployment. The first Spitfire flew in 1936.

ment, and soon Italian and German troops were helping Franco, and Russia was sending military aid to the "Popular Front" government. It was the marching of military jack-boots, not the depressed dragging of hob-nailed boots, that made the British government start to put money into the economy and thus create jobs for the unemployed. As had happened in 1931 with the Invergordon Mutiny, a military threat brought the right economic answer to an apparently insoluble problem. In March 1936, the National Government under Stanley Baldwin stepped up its plans for re-arming Britain, because of the growing threat from Hitler and Mussolini. The number of aeroplanes being built was already increasing (the Hurricane first flew in 1935 and the Spitfire in 1936), but now tanks, guns and ships were added to the list of projects on which the Government spent money and employed workers. Rearmament was a sad end to the hopes of the people who believed that war was gone for ever, but it was also the major step on the road to economic recovery. Ramsay MacDonald would probably never have taken the step, for he had spent most of his political life trying to bring peace, but he was a sick and sorrowful man who died in 1937 before he could see the population being issued with gas masks, and digging air-raid shelters in their gardens.

One other political figure who died before the full implications of rearmament became apparent was the King, George V. It may seem wrong to refer to the King as a political figure, but from the first days of his reign George V had been deeply involved in the running of the country and the Empire and Commonwealth. He had never run away from big issues; he helped to settle the argument over the Parliament Act of 1911; he appointed Prime Ministers in 1916, 1923, 1924 and 1931 when politicians were arguing amongst themselves and only he could resolve the problems; he brought together those who were arguing about the future of Ireland or of India, and he gave approval to a number of Acts of Parliament which were the beginnings of the "Welfare State" and of a new relationship between government and governed.

He had celebrated his Silver Jubilee in 1935. This was a new festival for the British people, for his grandmother Queen Victoria had only had Jubilee celebrations to mark the completion of fifty and sixty years on the throne. The decision to mark George's twenty-five years as King was deliberately taken, to give the British people something to cheer them up. They responded with unexpected warmth and enthusiasm, which almost overwhelmed their usually cool and rather gruff monarch. After he had driven in an open coach through the much

George V and Queen Mary drive through the East End
as part of their Jubilee celebrations.

The body of George V lies in state at Westminster.

decorated streets of the poorer parts of the East End of London, where he had been surrounded by adults and children cheering and singing and clapping, he admitted "I'd no idea they felt like that about me. I am beginning to think they like me for myself." They did. He had dignity, and calm strength. He was like a firm father (which indeed he was to his own children), but he had managed to appeal to the loyalty of his people. He was the first King to send a Christmas message to all his subjects on the "wireless", the first therefore to come as a living voice into their homes. On May 6th, 1935, he made a special Jubilee broadcast which showed just how moved he was. "How can I express what is in my heart? I can only say to you, my very very dear people, that the Queen and I thank you from the depths of our hearts for all the loyalty—and may I say so—the love, with which this day and always you have surrounded us. I dedicate myself anew to your service for all the years that may still be given me . . ."

There were no more full years to come. Just over eight months later, in January 1936, he died after a short illness. His last words were "How is the Empire?". His concern was typical of the man, and justified by the existing situation, for Britain was beginning the slide towards war that had been so dreaded since 1918.

CHAPTER EIGHT

World Wide   1901–1939

The Empire about which George V enquired just before his death was very different from the one he had inherited from his father in 1910, which in turn was markedly different from the Empire of 1901. Even while the words of *Land of Hope and Glory* were being written, Edward VII's Coronation was being postponed because of war within the Empire.

Turn the clock back to 1901, and look at Southern Africa. Barbed wire stretched for hundreds of miles across the dusty plains and scrubland; concrete blockhouses protected war-weary British soldiers who daily scoured the countryside for the remaining bands of Boer enemies. These farmers in their "commandoes" or small fighting bands, sneaked from area to area, raiding here and disrupting communications there, tweaking the tail of the imperial lion and fighting to the bitter end to avoid capture. The British responded by herding the Boer women and children into heavily guarded temporary accommodation which was soon to bring a new and dreadful phrase into the language—the "concentration camp". Inadequate food, bad water and overcrowding brought epidemics of measles, chicken-pox and dysentery to these camps, and twenty thousand women and children died in captivity there. The Boer War was struggling towards its conclusion, with victory at last going to the British army at the cost of frequent humiliation by the Boers' untrained but proud and deadly mounted marksmen. One of the few benefits to Britain of this war was that it made the War Office revise its organisation and training (and even uniform), and modernise the army through Haldane's Army Reforms, just as the experiences of the Crimean War had produced Cardwell's Army Reforms.

Another benefit was the production of a wise peace treaty, which was signed at Vereeniging in 1902. The object of the peace was to bring together the former Dutch and English settlers into a new nation of "South Africans", and by means of paying compensation for the damage inflicted on farms and livestock, and by granting full political rights to the defeated Boers and by

The Boer War. *Top:* Infantry crossing the Modder river in search of their elusive enemy. *Below:* Troops relaxing. Note the lamp and heliograph mirror for signalling before the days of radio.

winning the trust of the Boer leaders, a new "Union of South Africa" within the British Empire was created in a mere nine years. Men like Jan Smuts and Louis Botha who had resisted the British claims to Boer territory became loyal ministers of the British Crown in South Africa, and argued and even fought against other former Boer leaders who could not accept the new arrangements. Botha, the first Prime Minister of South Africa, conquered the German territory of South West Africa in 1914,

The peace negotiators at Vereeniging in 1902. The middle two in the front row are Botha (*left*) and Kitchener (*right*), then enemies but later to be allies against Germany in 1914.

and then sent volunteer South African troops to France and to East Africa. General Smuts, who was to succeed Botha as Prime Minister in 1919, was made part of Lloyd George's War Cabinet in 1917, a sign of his own personal greatness and of the success of the bond forged between former foes. It was also a sign of British reliance on the troops from the Dominions, who in total sent one and a quarter million men to the front in the First World War on Britain's behalf. It is often overlooked that Canada suffered more casualties in the war than did the United States of America, and that Australia's casualty rate was higher still in terms of its population, due largely to the horrors of the Gallipoli campaign.

In the history of the twentieth-century Empire, there is one outstanding man whose early political history is linked with South Africa but who became the true founder of the modern state of India. His name was Mohandas Gandhi.

Gandhi was born in India, and trained as a lawyer. He became a barrister in 1889, and left India to work in Southern Africa on behalf of the many Indians in that colony, whose dark skins brought them bad treatment from both Dutch and English settlers. Gandhi hated war and violence, not for any lack of courage, but because they did not seem to him to justify the evils

The Imperial allies; General Smuts of South Africa and the Maharajah of Bikaner inspecting English troops in London, 1917.

that followed them. He refused to fight for the British in the Boer War, though many of his fellow countrymen were brought from India for that purpose, but he ran a Red Cross unit which provided stretcher bearers and medical posts in several of the tougher battles. He and his men displayed great bravery as they rescued the wounded of either side, and he was officially commended for his work.

To be in the thick of a battle and yet not to be fighting was to become Gandhi's way of life. He never ran away from a struggle, but always preached non-violence, and began to practise what he preached when in 1913 the South African government passed a law limiting the rights of Indians to travel, trade, farm or hold property in the Union. Gandhi at once organised a peaceful march of 2,500 Indians from Natal into the Transvaal, to test their right to march from one province to another; he and other leaders were arrested, but this action was followed by strikes in various parts of the country, and eventually the South African government passed new laws which gave the Indians a larger amount of freedom than members of the black African tribes were allowed, though not as much as white men had. Gandhi however seemed satisfied, and returned to India in 1915.

The Coronation Durbar in Delhi, 1911; a reigning British monarch visits India for the first time.

India had enjoyed internal peace since the end of the Mutiny in 1858, when the East India Company had been forced by Act of Parliament to hand over control of the subcontinent to the Crown. In 1876 Victoria had been proclaimed Empress of India, a title which the Indians welcomed as much as she did, for it made them feel more intimately linked with Britain. In 1909 the Morley-Minto Reforms gave Indians a chance to elect their own countrymen to many of the advisory councils, and in 1911, just six months after the Coronation in England, George V and Queen Mary made the first-ever visit of a reigning British monarch to India. The Coronation Durbar at Delhi was a magnificent occasion, and the 80,000 people present heard the King-Emperor announce a host of new reforms. Delhi itself was to be the new capital, instead of the British-built Calcutta. All soldiers and civil servants were to have an extra month's pay, Indians were to be eligible to win the Victoria Cross for gallantry, fifty lacs of rupees (one lac equals one hundred thousand) were to be made available for the education of the people, and so on. The loyalty of the Indians to the British Crown had never been stronger, and nearly a million of them were to prove it by fighting for their "mother" country in the First World War.

After the war, a new Act of Parliament, based on the Montagu-

Indian troops at Gallipoli,
hauling a gun into position.

Chelmsford Report of 1918, introduced a system whereby the
Indians had even more say in their own government, but it came
too late to prevent trouble. Prices were high, there was an
epidemic of influenza which killed more people than the worst
famine in the last hundred years, and India was ablaze with hot-
headed ideas of complete self-government. Assassinations were
frequent, and local revolts were widespread. In Amritsar in the
Punjab, right in the north of the country, a mob got out of hand in
April 1919 and murdered four Europeans and burnt down all the
banks and government buildings. Military rule was declared
necessary, and three days later an English soldier, General Dyer,
found himself confronted by a huge threatening crowd which
refused to break up. After a brief hesitation, he ordered his small
force of fifty Indian troops to open fire. For ten minutes, volleys
rang out above the screams and curses of the frantic crowd. When
the scene cleared, nearly four hundred Indians lay dead, and
twelve hundred were wounded. It was an infamous massacre,
made even more humiliating for the Indians when, a week later,
Dyer ordered that all natives crossing a certain street in Amritsar
should do so on their hands and knees. Dyer was forced to resign
from the British Army, though there were many who felt that his
desperate display of force had prevented a new Mutiny from

Mohandas Gandhi in London for the Round Table Conference in 1931, with his spinning wheel.

breaking out. There is no doubt that calm gradually came back after Amritsar, but it was an ominous calm. Mohandas Gandhi saw to that.

Gandhi, remembering his success in South Africa, preached civil disobedience and non-cooperation. He ordered young Indians not to go to English-run schools, and not to use the law courts that were run by English judges. He suggested that no Indians should buy English cloth, but should spin and weave their own material; he adopted a spinning wheel as a symbol of his movement, and wherever he went, he took one with him. The English made fun of him and his wheel, but the Indians followed his words fanatically. He was like a prophet leading his people to a promised land; when the government reluctantly doubled the salt tax to try to reduce India's financial difficulties, Gandhi led a huge march 240 miles across India to Dandi beach where he defied the Government by taking from the sea, and tasting, a few grains of untaxed salt. He was sent to prison, and there he announced his intention of fasting until he died. Fifty thousand of his followers also ended up in gaol.

The British Government was stuck; they knew that India would sooner or later become a self-governing Dominion like Australia or Canada, but they could not be convinced that the time had come yet. The "Salt March" was in 1930. In 1929 Lord

116

Irwin, the Viceroy of India, had already promised Dominion status, but in 1930 a Commission led by Lord Simon reported that only provincial areas and not the central government were ready for Indian control. From 1930 to 1932, a series of "Round Table Conferences" was held, and Gandhi was let out of prison to attend the second one in London. Eventually a new "Government of India Act" was produced in 1935, which left most power in the hands of the British Viceroy, but did allow the Indians, particularly the princes, much more say in their own affairs. Gandhi was not satisfied. His party, Congress, cooperated with the British in one sense, but continued to work for Indian independence, which was finally achieved in 1947. In 1948, Gandhi the non-violent, Gandhi the "Mahatma" ("man of great soul") was assassinated by a Hindu who had once been his faithful follower.

South Africa, India and Ireland were the three areas of the world where British troops were used in the period 1901–1936 (not counting the many theatres of war in 1914–1918). British foreign policy in that period was devoted to two main principles only. The first was the peaceful reorganisation of the Empire, and the second was the maintenance of world peace after the horrors of the First World War.

The word "Dominion" has been used frequently in this chapter. It means simply "self-governing country" and it was first applied to the group of British North American colonies that became in 1867 the "Dominion of Canada". Australia became a Dominion in 1901, New Zealand in 1907 and the Union of South Africa in 1910. The Irish Free State had also had "Dominion status" since 1923, but no-one really knew what this meant. Another new idea that had come into common use was that of "the Commonwealth", but that too was undefined.

In 1931, Parliament passed the Statute of Westminster, which was a stepping stone in world history. Never before had an Empire voluntarily announced that it was going into equal partnership with the countries that it had once ruled. The

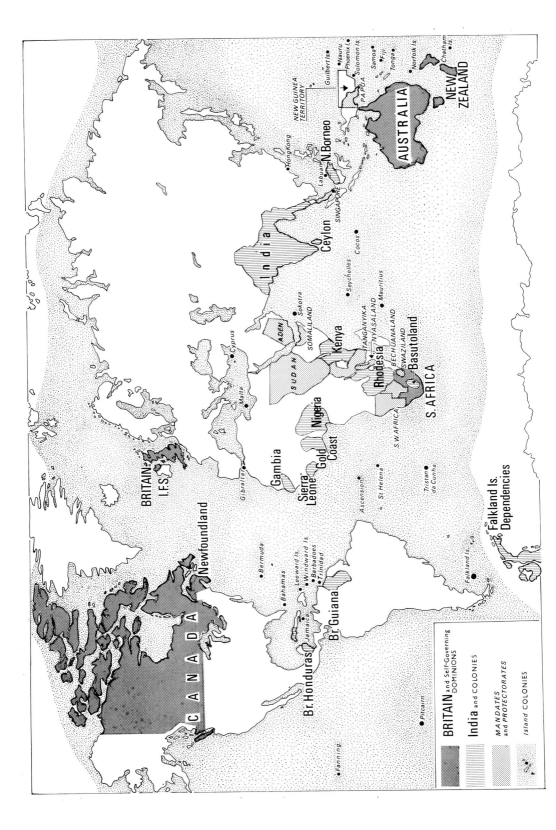

BRITAIN and Self-Governing DOMINIONS

India and COLONIES

MANDATES and PROTECTORATES

Island COLONIES

CANADA

Newfoundland

BRITAIN: I.F.S.

Gibraltar

Malta

Cyprus

Gambia

Sierra Leone

Gold Coast

Nigeria

SUDAN

ADEN

SOMALILAND

Sokotra

Kenya

TANGANYIKA

NYASALAND

Rhodesia

BECHUANALAND

SWAZILAND

S.W. AFRICA

Basutoland

S. AFRICA

India

Ceylon

Cocos

Seychelles

Mauritius

SINGAPORE

Labuan

N. Borneo

Hong Kong

NEW GUINEA TERRITORY

PAPUA

Guilbert Is.

Nauru

Phoenix Is.

Solomon Is.

Samoa

Fiji

Tonga

Norfolk Is.

Chatham Is.

AUSTRALIA

NEW ZEALAND

Br. Honduras

Br. Guiana

Bermuda

Bahamas

Jamaica

Leeward Is.

Windward Is.

Barbadoes

Trinidad

Ascension

St Helena

Tristan da Cunha

Falkland Is. Dependencies

Falkland Is.

Pitcairn

Fanning

complicated clauses of the Statute made it clear that Britain no longer claimed any control over its Dominions, though the British monarch was to be the Head of each of the new "Commonwealth" countries. Despite this, each country was to have its own elected government, its own laws and courts, and its own policies. When the Prime Ministers of the Dominions met, they were to be regarded as equal to each other, and equal to the Prime Minister of England, and it was hoped that the remaining "colonies" of the British Empire, which were mostly in Africa and the West Indies, would at some future date advance from their junior position into the partnership of the Commonwealth. The solidarity of the Commonwealth was put to an interesting test in 1939. When Britain declared war on Germany in that year, Australia and New Zealand immediately considered that they were at war too, South Africa remained neutral for five days and Canada for a week before individually declaring war on Hitler, while Eire, as the Irish Free State had called itself since 1937, declared itself neutral and remained so throughout the war. Eire later became the first country to leave the Commonwealth, which it did in 1949. Since 1947, when India and Pakistan became members as soon as they gained their independence, thirty nations have joined the partnership, and three have left (Eire, South Africa and (West) Pakistan).

The other great principle of British foreign policy after the First World War was to do everything possible for world peace. Although Lloyd George went to the Congress of Versailles in 1919 promising to squeeze Germany dry "until the pips squeaked" like those of an orange, what Britain really wanted was to be able to go back to what had been called "Splendid Isolation". She did not want binding alliances; she did not want another "scrap of paper" to force her into another bloody and brutal war; she wanted peace, trade and prosperity. She supported the League of Nations which was set up to solve international problems by agreement and not by force, and she was prepared to discuss disarmament at almost any time in the 1920s and early 1930s, though not always very practically. In 1927 Britain refused to agree to drop her number of cruisers below seventy, even though she had only fifty at that time, with no plans to build any more. In 1932 the R.A.F. refused to ban bombing in any future war, and the army refused to stop using the tank, which by many was believed to be the worst weapon that Man could devise. But these were mere details; in principle Britain supported disarmament and believed in what Churchill later called "jaw, jaw rather than war, war".

All the British Prime Ministers of the post-war period sought peace and a balanced Europe. Despite his tough words in England, Lloyd George tried to soften the punishment of Germany by his allies, refusing to allow the Saar to become a permanent part of France, and arguing against the creation of a huge Poland on the grounds that it would be a possible source of war with a resentful Germany later on. He was successful in these two things, though the price of the latter was a promise that, as a

The statesmen who tried to create permanent peace after the First World War: Clemenceau of France, Wilson of the U.S.A., and Lloyd George of Britain, at Versailles in 1919.

member of the League of Nations, Britain would take action if ever Poland were attacked. It was a price that Britain found herself called upon to pay in September 1939.

In 1924 Ramsay MacDonald organised a London Conference to sort out some of the financial problems of Western Europe and of Germany in particular, and in the same year he led a British delegation to Geneva which produced the idea, widely approved, that all international disputes *must* be solved by consultation and agreement, not by force. In 1925 the new Conservative Government refused to be bound by MacDonald's "Geneva Protocol", but instead signed the Locarno Treaties, in which Germany promised not to go to war in order to change her frontiers, and the other major European powers agreed to make sure that this promise was kept. In 1928, the same Conservative Government, led by Stanley Baldwin, signed the Kellogg-Briand Peace Pact, by which virtually every country promised not to go to war except in self-defence. Peace seemed to be assured, and even after the Wall Street crash of 1929, when financial and political tension returned to Europe, England was apparently determined to stay out of trouble.

In February 1933, in a debate in the Oxford Union, members of the University passed by a large majority the motion that "this House will never again fight for King and Country". They were not being disloyal; they simply believed in the necessity of continued peace. In October 1933, in a by-election in East Fulham, the Labour candidate won the Parliamentary seat with a majority of 5,000 whereas two years earlier the seat had been held by a Conservative with a 14,000 majority. The great switch of votes was said to have been because the Labour candidate was a "Peace" candidate. Only one politician of the time firmly argued against disarmament, and against the "Peace at any price" attitude, and he was Winston Churchill, unpopular in his own party for his outspoken and embarrassing views, and disliked or distrusted by M.P.s and voters in the other parties. His voice rasped on unheard or unheeded, while in 1935, European events

121

The sign of a shrinking world. Alan Cobham flies over Westminster after a record-breaking solo flight from Australia in 1926.

took a sinister turn. In April, MacDonald of Britain, Mussolini of Italy and Laval of France met at Stresa to confirm their belief in peace, but Mussolini's troops were already clashing with Abyssinians in north-east Africa, and MacDonald was about to negotiate a naval treaty with Germany which allowed Hitler to build surface ships and submarines despite all the rulings of the Treaty of Versailles and the Disarmament Conferences.

Worse was to come. In December 1935 Sir Samuel Hoare, the Foreign Secretary, made an agreement with Laval of France that Britain and France would allow Italy to invade and keep the fertile plains of Abyssinia if Italy would allow the Emperor of Abyssinia to keep a small kingdom in the mountains. The plan leaked out, and public opinion suddenly turned against peace at any price, and became angry with Hoare, who resigned, and with the whole Government, who simply blamed Hoare. The League of Nations was shown to be useless, a fact which Hitler knew when in March 1936 he sent German troops back into the "de-militarised" zone of the Rhineland.

All Churchill's warnings were coming true, and slowly, the British people came to the sad realisation that peace cannot be forced onto a country or a leader that does not want it. For three more years, while they began to hurry to produce tanks, guns, ships and aircraft, British politicians tried to secure "peace with honour" in negotiations with Hitler and Mussolini. On September 1st, 1939, German troops advanced into Poland as their bombers growled overhead to blitz Warsaw. Britain warned Hitler that if he did not withdraw within twenty-four hours, Britain would declare war on Germany, but no withdrawal came. As Neville Chamberlain, the Prime Minister, told the House of Commons on September 3rd "This country is at war with Germany . . . Everything that I have worked for, everything that I have hoped for, everything that I have believed in during my public life, has crashed into ruins". So had British foreign policy of the past twenty years. It was left for Winston Churchill to come to power in 1940 to pull together the joint might of the Commonwealth and Empire, and to combine with American, Russian and European allies to crush the double-headed monster of Nazism and Fascism.

CHAPTER NINE

The Age of Communication   1901–1939

In 1910 Dr Crippen of Liverpool murdered his wife and fled from justice in England by going to Brussels. From there he decided to go to Canada, and with his secretary, he took ship under the assumed name of Mr Robinson, accompanied by his "son". As his liner, the S.S. *Montrose,* left the English Channel and headed out into the Atlantic, Crippen must have felt safe, but he was about to play the central role in a drama that made international news.

The captain of the *Montrose* was suspicious about Mr Robinson and his "son", and when 150 miles off the Lizard lighthouse, he had tapped out his suspicions in Morse code on his new wireless equipment. No reply was received, probably because his equipment was too weak to pick up the signal, but a few days later, his wireless operator overheard a strong signal beamed to another ship, the *Laurentic,* which was slowly overhauling the *Montrose* on the long route across the ocean. The signal made it clear that Inspector Dew of Scotland Yard was aboard the *Laurentic,* and that he would get to Canada first. As the *Montrose* entered the St Lawrence Seaway, a small boat came out from shore bringing a "pilot". but when once aboard the *Montrose,* the pilot revealed himself as Inspector Dew; he arrested Crippen, who was taken back to England, found guilty of murder, and executed.

This triumph for modern techniques came only nine years after Marconi had himself crossed the Atlantic by ship, and from the coast of Newfoundland had flown a kite bearing an aerial wire to 4,000 feet. Then, hunched over a primitive receiver, he had clearly heard the three short dots of the Morse letter S being signalled from Cornwall nearly two thousand miles away. How the signal managed to reach him despite the curvature of the earth he did not fully understand, but he had proved that such a thing could happen, and within a few years all ships were being equipped with wireless. Ships were the obvious vehicles to make full use of the heavy transmitting and receiving apparatus, and its worth was proved not only by the arrest of Crippen in 1910, but also by the rescue of 1,500 people from two ships which collided

Marconi demonstrates some of his early 'wireless' equipment.

off the coast of America and sank. Thanks to the wireless operator's bravery, no life was lost save those who suffered in the collision itself.

Two years later, the passengers of the *Titanic* were not so fortunate as they were further from land and in icy waters when their ship sank. *Titanic* was the world's largest and "safest" ship; indeed it was claimed that she was unsinkable. On her maiden voyage from Southampton to New York, in April 1912, she was packed with the wealthy of the western world; the magnificence of her 50,000 tons amazed everyone and she was considered to be a floating palace, filled with every luxury and fitted with every modern device. Five nights from Southampton, travelling

Survivors of the *Titanic* disaster in their lifeboat.

What the coming of the radio meant to ordinary people; photograph taken in a village pub in 1941, when Churchill was addressing the nation.

at $22\frac{1}{2}$ knots, she sliced into an iceberg and tore a hole a hundred yards long in her side at and below the waterline. Two hours later she sank; two hours after that, the liner *Carpathia*, summoned from 60 miles away by wireless distress signals, arrived to rescue seven hundred of the passengers and crew from the numbing waters. Over fifteen hundred others were dead or missing.

Wireless did not long remain just a safety feature on ships. It was something that could be adapted so that private houses could have their own receiving sets, though the British Post Office was at first reluctant to allow this to happen. It was not until 1920 that they authorised the transmission of speech rather than Morse Code, and in 1922 the British Broadcasting Company was set up at Marconi House in London, with the call sign "This is 2L0, London calling". Broadcasts did not reach very far, and there were some peculiar features about them. When dance bands played music, they came to a studio which had just one microphone suspended from the centre of the ceiling, and dancing couples, provided to add atmosphere, jostled to get under the microphone and call out greetings to any friends who might be "listening in". One microphone used in 1925 was so sensitive that it had to be covered with cloth, and even so a singer with a powerful voice had to stand up to forty feet away from it.

During the General Strike of 1926, when newspapers ceased for ten days, the British Broadcasting Company took on a new

John Logie Baird, with his television camera and transmitter. What he invented was originally called 'wireless vision'.

importance with its regular announcements about what was happening, and by 1927 over a million households had receivers. In that year, the Company became the British Broadcasting Corporation, under the continued direction of Sir John Reith, and the range of its broadcasts grew in every sense, though there was only one main channel with a few regional transmitters until the Second World War when the "Forces Network" was added to the "Home Service". By 1936 the regular features included "Children's Hour", Schools' programmes, music of all sorts, plays, serials and news broadcasts, and in 1936 the B.B.C. also began the world's first public television service. It had a range of 45 miles in the best weather conditions, and viewers had to look at a screen less than a foot across, on which crude pictures were made up of 180 lines of moving dots (compared with the 625 lines on modern sets). The man who had pioneered this technical revolution was John Logie Baird, who died in 1946 before his invention had been perfected and made available to the ordinary household.

Before radio and television, but after the majority of people had learned to read and write, the main source of communication was the newspaper. In Victorian times, this had been something for the upper classes only, with *The Times* and the *Morning Post* aiming to educate the educated. In 1896, however, Alfred Harmsworth, later Lord Northcliffe, who had started his career as

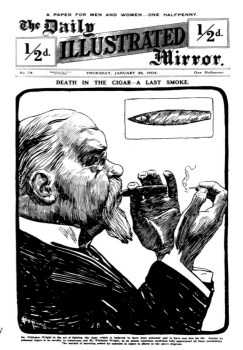

The first issue of the *Daily Illustrated Mirror*, 1904.

a reporter on the Hampstead and Highgate Express, launched a new style of paper, *The Daily Mail*. Northcliffe was full of new ideas, and the *Daily Mail* reported things of all sorts that had escaped the attention of the editors of the older newspapers. "Written by office boys for office boys" was the sniffy verdict of Lord Salisbury, the Prime Minister, but within three years, the *Mail* had a daily circulation of over half a million copies, easily the largest in the country. In 1903, Northcliffe tried another fresh approach: he brought out the *Daily Mirror*, "written by gentlewomen for gentlewomen". It was a terrible flop, and so in 1904 he changed its name and its style to the *Daily Illustrated Mirror*, "for men and women, the first halfpenny daily illustrated publication in the history of journalism". This time it succeeded, and together with the *Mail* it captured a new host of regular readers. The papers sponsored races for motor cars and aeroplanes; they reported sport fully; they ran pages for women, and campaigns for social improvement; whatever they did, they sought and gave publicity in a new, deliberately challenging way. Men like Northcliffe and later Max Aitken (Lord Beaverbrook) created power for themselves when they created the "New Journalism", and with this power they were able to influence public taste and popular ideas about politics and

An airliner of the 1930s.

progress, fashions and football, women and wars. They were the new communicators, who brought up-to-date knowledge within reach of anyone in the land, in language that anyone could understand.

Communication was not just a matter of words in a paper or on the wireless. Other technical advances were shrinking the world's distances to relatively insignificant amounts, often with the encouragement of Lord Northcliffe. The Wright brothers made the first ever flight in a heavier-than-air machine in 1903. It lasted for fifty-nine seconds. In 1906 Europe saw its first powered flight, and the *Daily Mail* was offering a prize of £150 for the best power-driven model aircraft. In 1908 came the first powered flight in England, and in 1909 Bleriot crossed the Channel by air to win Northcliffe's £1,000 prize for doing so. His flight lasted twenty-seven minutes. A *Daily Mail* prize of £10,000 was won in 1910 for flying from London to Manchester, another in 1911 for a Circuit of Britain Race, another in 1919 by Alcock and Brown for achieving the first Atlantic crossing. In 1927 the American Captain Lindbergh flew from New York to Paris, the first solo crossing of the Atlantic, and in 1928 the world speed record was pushed above 300 m.p.h. for the first time. By 1930 aeroplanes and airships had the capability to go almost anywhere in the world, and designers knew enough to build airliners or bombers, seaplanes or fighters as required. Reginald Mitchell, the chief designer for a company called Supermarine Aviation, designed the high-speed seaplanes that won the international Schneider Trophy for Britain four times, and before he died in 1937 he had adapted the design of his latest seaplane and produced the Supermarine Spitfire, which first flew in 1936.

Meanwhile road transport was also coming into its own. Back in 1865 the Government had decreed that "road engines" must go no faster than four miles per hour, and must be preceded by a man on foot with a warning red flag. This law was softened in 1896, but from 1903 until 1930, 20 m.p.h. was the maximum legal speed; after that, 30 m.p.h. was the maximum speed allowed in built-up areas, but there was no top speed limit on the open road until the 1960s.

The first all-British four-wheeled car was produced in 1896, by a young man called Herbert Austin; in 1903 the Vauxhall Company came in to production, and in 1904 Henry Royce and Charles Rolls started a partnership which dedicated itself to producing the highest standard of engineering possible. While other cars were produced for economy in order to compete with the mass-produced models from Henry Ford's American factories, the Rolls-Royce Company staked its future on quality, and its "Silver Ghost" of 1906 was so far ahead of its time that it was produced without significant change for a further nineteen years.

Early motoring was hazardous. Cars were difficult to start, and if you were trying to start a Model T Ford in cold weather in about 1910, you were advised to jack the rear wheels off the ground. If you failed to do so, and then swung the starting handle at the front of the car, either of two things could happen: the car could backfire, spinning the starting handle in the wrong direction and threatening to break your wrist, or it could start properly and immediately move forward because of cold, stiff oil in the gear box, thereby running over its indignant driver. Brake

130

failure was another peril, and even as late as 1920, some cars were fitted with "sprags", which were hinged spikes attached to the rear axle. If a car seemed to be running away downhill, the wise driver released his sprag which would dig into the road like an anchor, and bring the car to a halt.

There were other, more human perils. At first it was unclear which side of the road the car should occupy, but eventually the recommendation of a Lancashire court back in 1795 that "coach-men, postilions, waggoners and carters" should always keep to the left became the accepted practice, and in the 1920s, white lines were first drawn in the centre of the roads to increase safety. Another human hazard was the policeman who set traps to catch speeding motorists. An ingenious answer to this problem came from a group of intrepid motorists who formed the "Automobile Association" and paid for "scouts" to travel along the major roads by bicycle or motorcycle. The "scouts" had two jobs. One was to help to repair members' cars that broke down, but the other was to discover the whereabouts of police speed traps. If a trap was found, the scout stationed himself further along the road, and, instead of saluting when a member's car went past him, he stayed motionless. The A.A. member would stop his car to reprimand the scout, and the scout could then explain his deliberate rudeness, and warn the motorist not to drive too fast.

There were also fears that driving was a lazy habit, bad for the health. It was seriously suggested that after driving twenty miles or so, one should stop and go for a brisk run of about three hundred yards lest one's leg muscles, so important in a horse-riding era, should get weak. But horse-riding days were over. More and more firms were set up to produce cars, one famous one starting in a cycle shop in Cowley, a suburb of Oxford, where W. R. Morris changed from building bicycles to motorcycles and ultimately to cars. Starting with a capital of £4, Morris built up a huge fortune, giving £4,000,000 to medical research, at least another £4,000,000 to other charities, and at least £2,000,000 in shares to his own work force. He was created Viscount Nuffield in

131

Racing at Brooklands in 1923.
Malcolm Campbell driving a Peugeot.

1938, and amongst his memorials is a college named after him in the University of Oxford.

Many of the improvements in motor cars came from research done by people interested in racing and competing with each other. The most famous racetrack in England was established at Brooklands in 1907, where steeply banked curves encouraged more and more speed. By the early 1920s some cars could exceed 100 m.p.h., and record-breakers had to seek a long flat surface on which to get their vehicles up to full speed and stop again in safety. Most went to Daytona Beach in Florida, and the 1922 record of 134 m.p.h. went up to 231 m.p.h. in 1929, 272 m.p.h. in 1931, and in 1935 to 301 m.p.h., with Sir Malcolm Campbell at the wheel of his new streamlined 2,500 horsepower *Bluebird*. This was much faster than many aircraft could fly.

The last word about speed must mention the railways, which reached their peak in the period 1901–1936, before road and air competition began to bite into their activities. Speed was not given as much emphasis as safety and reliability, and although the *Mallard* became the fastest steam engine in the world when it reached 126 m.p.h. in 1938, the railway companies were looking at new developments—diesel engines, automatic signalling, long distance electrification, even overhead monorails. Comfort, convenience and service to the passenger were all more important to railwaymen than sheer speed, and the British Isles enjoyed a network of railway lines which sometimes reached into the smallest villages.

132

Campbell's car in 1935; 'Bluebird', which took the land speed record above 300 m.p.h.

This typified the revolution that was going on in communications. What was new in this age was that every man's world had been widened as far as the train, plane or car would carry him and every news item could be spread as far as wireless or the popular press could reach. Britain in the last quarter of the nineteenth century had prided herself on her "Splendid Isolation", but now such a thing did not exist in foreign policy and certainly could not exist in the realm of ideas and attitudes. Ordinary people were exposed to fads and fashions which swept across the civilised world, changing their music, their reading, their entertainments, their clothes, their whole way of life. The affairs of the world were being stirred together in one huge cauldron, and advantages and disadvantages slopped out indiscriminately. New techniques discovered on one continent were snatched up by another, and the pace of life quickened remorselessly. New machines took the place of human labour, and automation became a process which brought both hope of a better world and fear of unemployment. "Time is money", said Henry Ford, and his assembly-line factories were copied by businessmen involved in all sorts of production. The population of the world was growing rapidly; it had more skill, more education and knowledge, more say in its own affairs, more wealth and more leisure. Its eyes, ears and brain were opened in this age of communication.

Because there was more wealth and more leisure, this was a golden age of entertainment, and the greatest novelty in

133

Spreading a new craze; fashionable ladies learn to charleston.

entertainment in the first quarter of the century was the moving picture. Just who invented it is still a matter of dispute, and the truth probably is that several men were trying out different systems at the same time. An Englishman, Friese-Green, demonstrated "cinematography" in 1885 and patented a film camera in 1889, the same year in which Edison announced his "kinetoscope" in America. Early film-shows were very short affairs, lasting perhaps one minute in a tiny tent in a fairground alongside "The Bearded Lady" or "The Smallest Man in the World" or some other imaginative freak, and it was not until 1904 that Britain had its first permanent cinema, the Daily Bioscope at Bishopsgate in London. Equipment was primitive—one projector operator set up a lavatory cistern over his machine so that if it burst into flames, he merely had to pull the chain—and in 1908 sixteen children were trampled to death in Barnsley in the panic which resulted from a fire in a cinematograph exhibition. Not only were the films short but they were also often fakes. Action pictures of the signing of the Peace of Vereeniging in South Africa in 1902 were actually taken at Loughborough Junction.

Early films were accompanied by a pianist who played music suitable for the scene on the screen, romantic, dramatic or tension-building as the need arose, and sometimes a sound-effects man sat near the screen with coconut shells to imitate hoof-beats, and sandpaper to scrape together to make a watery sound. From 1904 onwards it was possible to see a moving picture show with sound which came from a gramophone record, but there was

The cinema idol—
Mary Pickford
in the 1920s.

always a danger that the film and the record were going at different speeds, so that the heroine announced "her" passionate love in a deep voice, while the male star sounded squeaky and shy. Such embarrassments could be put right by slowing up the film or the gramophone by hand, which could produce a strange visual or aural effect, but the audiences did not mind. In 1928, the Warner Brothers studio made the first full length film with the sound track actually on the film so that problems of synchronisation were over, but "when the handle of the door turned I thought someone had cranked up a farm tractor, and when the door closed it sounded like the collision of two lumber trucks. At the beginning they knew nothing about controlling sound: a knight-errant clanged like the noise in a steel factory, a simple family dinner sounded like the rush hour in a cheap restaurant. I came away from the theatre believing the days of sound were numbered". The man who wrote those words was not unfamiliar with films himself; his name was Charlie Chaplin.

Charlie Chaplin, English-born but destined to spend most of his working life in America, was one of the stars who was a brilliant success in both silent and talking films, though his silent comedies are the better remembered parts of his work. With his baggy trousers, bowler hat and cane, and his toes-out, knees-out walk, he was one of the earliest stars. The 1920s were more dominated by Mary Pickford, "the world's sweetheart", and by the handsome Italian idol, Rudolf Valentino. When he died at the age of 31 in 1926, hundreds of women went into deep mourning,

Cinema architecture.
The Granada at Tooting in 1937.

and his funeral could have been mistaken for a royal occasion at least.

Chaplin was wrong about the "talkies". They became more and more popular, sucking the audiences out of the theatres and the music halls, and, with colour film and lavish productions, shown in newly styled and extravagant buildings, they could create such a fantasy world that Hollywood, the centre of the industry, became known as "the Dream Factory".

Another import from America which spread rapidly was a new style and spirit of music which was generally called "jazz". Originally known as "ragtime" and producing the first international "hit" tune in *Alexander's Ragtime Band,* it gripped the young of Britain in the 1920s, and could be heard blaring out from gramophones, the wireless, dance halls and private parties. It made popular a new range of instruments like the banjo, the ukelele, the saxophone and the trumpet, and it produced a series of high-kicking dances of which the Charleston is the best remembered. It symbolised the new freedoms of the young; it was associated with the "flappers" with their skirts above their knees, their lipstick and powder and long cigarette holders, their

Guests arrive at a Buckingham Palace Garden Party in 1926, and the hem-lines show how fashion is changing with the generations.

discussion of things that their mothers would never have thought about, let alone discussed. It was fast and free-flowing, a triumphant claim to a brave new world where the old ideas and values were being thrust aside by a new wave of energetic "bright young things". And because it happened in the midst of the great communications revolution, it was a new phenomenon which some people found frightening or shocking. "For God's sake let us be men, not monkeys minding machines or sitting with our tails curled while the machine amuses us, the radio or film or gramophone," wrote D. H. Lawrence. Ironically he too was considered shocking, and although he influenced other men of letters, his novels and poems were not widely accepted in the 1920s.

The 1920s were a high point of hope, laughter, gaiety and change. New things came and went, shining brilliantly for a while, and giving way to something else. But as the world moved into the 1930s, with its intertwined threads of poverty, unemployment, depression and fear of war, a dark and sober mood crept into English life. Optimism paled in front of cold economic facts and political tangles, and the decade started to slide down a rough and treacherous path towards war. Not all the communication in the world could prevent the descent, and at times it hastened it by turning truth into lies and ideas into arguments.

CHAPTER TEN

One King and One Commoner   1936

At 9.30 on the evening of January 19th, 1936, British broadcasts were interrupted suddenly; there was a pause, long enough to draw the listeners' attention. Then "London calling the British Empire. The King's life is drawing peacefully to a close." The message was repeated every quarter of an hour, until, just after midnight, it was announced that George V, the first King to use the wireless in order to speak to his people, had died in his sleep.

The sadness of the moment was offset by one acknowledged fact. Edward Albert Christian George Andrew Patrick David, George V's eldest son, was the most popular and respected heir to the throne for centuries. He had been invested Prince of Wales at Caernarvon Castle within a month of his father's Coronation, and he had from that moment been trained for the arduous job of kingship that would inevitably become his upon his father's death. He had set out to know his people and to be known by them. In the First World War he had visited the trenches in the front lines, only to return to his car to find it riddled with German shrapnel and his driver dead. He went on to serve in Egypt and in Italy, and when the war was over, he toured Newfoundland, Canada and the United States, then Australia, New Zealand and the West Indies, and then India, Singapore and Hong Kong, all with great success despite the efforts of Gandhi to upset the Indian tour. The personality of Prince Edward broke through the sullen welcomes which he sometimes received in India, and he was a brilliant ambassador for Britain and for the Crown. He was young, handsome, sensible but not stuffy, and sensitive to the people whom he met. He preferred to meet men and women of his own age, and sometimes cut formal meetings to their barest bones, which offended some of the older figures, but he was recognised as a straightforward and honest man.

He got himself into trouble sometimes with his stern father, George V. His 1924 tour of the United States of America was a social success, but soon a letter was on its way from the King in Balmoral Castle. "According to the daily telegrams in the papers you must be having a pretty strenuous time, as besides playing

The Prince with the
film star image;
a postcard from
the 1920s.

polo and various other things in the day at most of which you are
mobbed, you dance until 6 o'clock every morning, including Sun-
days. It's a pity the Press can't be induced to leave you alone . . .''.
When Edward returned to England, his first meeting with
his father was icy. The King had on his desk a heap of American
newspaper cuttings with glaring headlines: PRINCE GETS IN
WITH MILKMAN; HERE HE IS, GIRLS—THE MOST ELIGIBLE
BACHELOR YET UNCAUGHT; and OH! WHO'LL ASK H.R.H.
WHAT HE WEARS ASLEEP. It was the sort of publicity that the
English Royal Family hated.

Even when Edward was trying to do something for ordinary
people caught by the Depression in England and in his own
Principality of Wales, he was criticised by the Government and
impatient with his own powerlessness. In his own story, he wrote
how he visited Tyneside. "Few ships were built, but the people
remained—there was no work or home for them elsewhere.
Walking about the dismal cottages on the riverbank, I came upon
a man. He was about forty, poorly but cleanly dressed, erect and
with an honest face. 'What is your trade?' I asked. 'Foreman
riveter, Sir,' he answered. 'How long is it since you have
worked?' 'Five years, Sir.' His eyes searched mine. Manifestly he
expected me, the King's son, to be able to offer him some hope.
But what response could I make . . .? That the Monarchy was not
responsible for his plight? That the Government was doing all it
could? That he had only to be patient? What possible solace

139

Left: Edward, Prince of Wales, meeting working men in 1919.
Right: King Edward VIII on Armistice Day, 1936, four weeks before his Abdication.

would that have given to a man who had been on the dole for five years?'' There were many aspects of being a member of the Royal Family that brought despair to the future king.

In 1931, Edward met an American couple at a weekend hunting party, though the wife, Mrs Wallis Simpson, was not interested in riding and hunting, and the conversation that she had with the Prince of Wales was brief. However she had already been presented at Court, and it was unsurprising that Edward should meet the Simpsons again, and become friendly with them. They had a flat in Bryanston Square in London, and Edward would drop in on them from time to time. By 1935, Edward, "the most eligible bachelor yet uncaught" was aware of the fact that he loved Wallis Simpson, and that he was therefore in an impossible situation. He wanted to talk it over with the King, his father, but George V was under great strain and indeed was a dying man. The conversation never took place, though if it had, it could not have changed the circumstances. It was virtually impossible for Edward to marry Mrs Simpson.

The English monarch is also Governor of the Church of England and has the extra title of Defender of the Faith. In the 1930s, divorce, though growing less uncommon, was something which was still frowned upon in Society, and it was only very recently that the *innocent* person in a divorce suit had been accepted at Court at all. Mrs Simpson had already divorced one husband, who was still alive, and she now wished to divorce Ernest Simpson. Technically she would be free to marry again, but Edward, though a bachelor, was not so free. He could if he wished marry a commoner, though it would have been unusual; he could if he wished marry an American, though America was a republican country. What he could not do was to marry an American commoner who would have twice divorced previous husbands. It was not against the law, but it would be against the whole spirit of the Monarchy and of the Church of England.

When George V died and Edward Prince of Wales became King Edward VIII, the nation knew little or nothing of the bitter conflict between love and duty that raged in the new King's heart. Wallis Simpson's name was mentioned occasionally on the Court page of the main newspapers when she attended formal dinner parties, but the English newspaper editors decided amongst themselves that they did not want to print gossip or scandal about the couple. French and American papers bristled with rumours, but few ordinary men and women travelled abroad in those days, and the rumours remained locked up in the minds of the wealthier and more aristocratic members of society.

For six months the King worked hard at his new job. There were ambassadors to see, people to meet, papers to sign. Eventually in the summer of 1936, he chartered a large yacht, and went cruising off the Dalmatian coast for a rest. Mrs Simpson was a guest on board, and during those few weeks, Edward became more than ever convinced that he wanted to marry her, and could not fulfil his job as King without her by his side. Not long after their return from the cruise, Mrs Simpson divorced her husband, and at the same time the Prime Minister, Stanley Baldwin, began to tell Edward of his worries about the future of the Monarchy if the King were to marry her. There were three possible courses of action: the King could give up the idea of marrying Mrs Simpson;

141

INSTRUMENT OF ABDICATION

   I, Edward the Eighth, of Great
Britain, Ireland, and the British Dominions
beyond the Seas, King, Emperor of India, do
hereby declare My irrevocable determination
to renounce the Throne for Myself and for
My descendants, and My desire that effect
should be given to this Instrument of
Abdication immediately.

   In token whereof I have hereunto set
My hand this tenth day of December, nineteen
hundred and thirty six, in the presence of
the witnesses whose signatures are subscribed.

SIGNED AT
FORT BELVEDERE
IN THE PRESENCE
OF

Above: The Instrument of Abdication; December
1936.
Right: The Duke and Duchess of Windsor after
their wedding in France, 1937.

or he could marry her morganatically (i.e., legally, but she would only become Mrs Windsor, and never Queen, and their children would never inherit the throne); or, finally, he could abdicate.

Edward himself was swinging towards the last choice, but Stanley Baldwin insisted that the opinion of the Dominions' Governments should be sought, as they too came under the British Crown. At that delicate moment, the long-dreaded storm of publicity in Britain broke. It was started by a speech by the Bishop of Bradford, who publicly criticised Edward's lack of church-going, and spoke of his need for God's guidance. It was a mild speech, but it got the headlines in the *Yorkshire Post* and other northern papers on December 2nd 1936, and it meant that the London papers could no longer keep their self-imposed silence. On December 3rd, the whole world knew the secret and the problem, and Wallis Simpson slipped discreetly away to France so that the King could take the final decisions uninfluenced by her presence.

Anxiously he watched public opinion as expressed in the newspapers. There was shock, dismay, distrust, and sometimes sympathy. The picture was not clear. But Baldwin and the Government had only one opinion; the King must abdicate, or they would resign. Despite an effort by Winston Churchill to get everyone to think again, the House of Commons hardened its heart against the marriage to Mrs Simpson, and Edward had no alternatives left to him. He abdicated on December 10th 1936, just nine days after the Bishop of Bradford had made his speech. The country, still reeling from the shock of the first news, was stunned.

Edward, freed from the gag of Kingship, gave his one and only broadcast about his decision on the night of December 11th. The text was simple, dignified and moving, and it ended with a pledge of allegiance to the new King, his own brother. After the broadcast, Edward said goodbye to his family and drove through the darkness to Portsmouth, from where a Royal Navy destroyer took him across the Channel. In 1937, Edward, now Duke of

143

Windsor, and Wallis Simpson were married quietly in France. They never lived permanently in England again.

On May 12th, 1937, the day appointed for the Coronation of Edward VIII, his younger brother George VI stood in his place. The nervous young man who had protested "I never wanted this to happen; I'm quite unprepared for it; I'm only a naval officer" took the vows that Edward would have taken, and dedicated the rest of his life to reign over Britain and its Empire and Commonwealth. There had been no disastrous collapse of the established order of things and the new King had the support and sympathy of his people. For Kings and for Commoners, life had to go on.

George VI, Princess Margaret, Princess (now Queen) Elizabeth, and Queen Elizabeth (now the Queen Mother). The Coronation portrait, 1937.

Index and Acknowledgements

Index

Figures in bold type denote pictures

Acknowledgements

Acknowledgements are listed in the order
in which the pictures appear.
A painting by Jacomb-Hood of King
George V and Queen Mary at the Delhi
Durbar: reproduced by gracious permission
of Her Majesty Queen Elizabeth II. Colour
plate.
Awaiting the funeral squadron.
Queen Victoria's funeral procession at
Windsor.
Edward, Prince of Wales.
Edward VII at Sandringham.
George V on horseback: by courtesy of Fox
Photos Ltd.
Edward VII and his Queen.
Edward Elgar.
Discovery.
Henley Regatta 1914.
Piccadilly Circus 1912.
Day Dress 1905.
Primary Education 1908.
Keir Hardie election poster.
Slum children 1910.
Herbert Asquith.
Archduke Franz Ferdinand and his wife
1914.
Wilhelm II Emperor of Germany 1900.
George V.
Nicholas II His Imperial Majesty The
Emperor of Russia.
Launching of HMS *Dreadnought* 1906.
Map of The Western Front, drawn by
E. H. A. Rennick.
British troops at Victoria Station.
Worcestershire Regiment.
Painting of an English charge at Laon.
Big Bertha.
Devastation near Verdun 1916.
Five war posters 1915.
'Call to Arms' poster.
'It is far better to face the bullets' poster:
by courtesy of Lords Gallery.
'Your country needs You' poster: by
courtesy of the Imperial War Museum.
Battle of the Somme 1916: by courtesy of
the Imperial War Museum.
Horse-drawn water cart: by courtesy of the
Imperial War Museum.
Tank in action on Western Front.
British troops resting.
French ambulance dog.
American nurse.
Souvenir from the First World War: by
courtesy of Mrs. B. Dix. Colour plate.
Map of Europe, drawn by E. H. A.

Rennick.
T. E. Lawrence.
Gallipoli, Anzac beach
HMS *Dreadnought* underway 1911.
German painting of the return from
Jutland.
British aircraft.
Drawing of German airmen.
Poster: 'Flying at Hendon': by courtesy of
London Transport. Colour plate.
British War Library 1916.
R.100 saloon.
R.101 circling St. Paul's Cathedral.
Twisted framework of R.101.
Mrs. Pankhurst with daughter Christabel.
Suffragettes at Buckingham Palace.
Forcible feeding poster.
Emily Davison's death at Epsom Derby.
Emily Davison's funeral.
Women bus conductors.
Women's fire service.
Sir Roger Casement.
Eamonn De Valera.
Painting of General Post Office, Dublin: by
courtesy of the National Museum of
Ireland.
General Post Office, Dublin after Easter
Rising.
London Cabaret.
Pawn shop 1921.
Perfect spirit iron: by courtesy of the Army
and Navy Stores Ltd.
Patent gas iron: by courtesy of the Army
and Navy Stores Ltd.
Kent's knife machine: by courtesy of the
Army and Navy Stores Ltd.
Wilcox & Gibbs' stitch machine: by
courtesy of the Army and Navy Stores Ltd.
'Iceland' portable refrigerator: by courtesy
of the Army and Navy Stores Ltd.
ABC Dinner Stove: by courtesy of the
Army and Navy Stores Ltd.
Red Star Washing Machine: by courtesy of
the Army and Navy Stores Ltd.
David Lloyd George 1919.
Stanley Baldwin 1922.
Labour Government 1924.
'Safety first' poster 1924.
Coal strike at Wigan 1921.
Pit pony, Wigan 1921.
Strikers football match 1926.
Food convoy at Hyde Park 1926.
Escort in East India Dock Road.

Volunteer driving Tram 1926.
Driver and Omnibus protected 1926.
Punch cartoon: Children: by courtesy of
Punch.
Flapper smoking 1920s.
Girl motor-cyclists 1925.
Car factory at Cowley 1930.
Qualified unemployed 1930's.
Sir Oswald Mosley 1932.
Unemployed man, Wigan 1939.
Punch cartoon: Vote! by courtesy of *Punch.*
Daily Mirror reporting Invergordon
Mutiny: by courtesy of Syndication
International Ltd.
Jarrow Crusade.
Spitfire.
Jubilee drive 1935.
George V lying in State.
Crossing the Modder river.
Troops relaxing with signalling equipment.
British commander with Boer envoys.
General Smuts with Maharajah of Bikaner
1917.
Troops massed for Delhi Durbar 1911.
Gallipoli, Walker Ridge 1915.
Mohandas Gandhi.
Map of the World, drawn by E. H. A.
Rennick.
Clemenceau, Wilson and Lloyd George
1919.
Alan Cobham over Westminster 1926.
Guglielmo Marconi.
Titanic survivors.
Listening to Churchill 1941.
John L. Baird and his television.
Daily Illustrated Mirror: by courtesy of
Syndication International Ltd.
Imperial Airways 'Hengist'.
Malcolm Campbell 1923.
Bluebird 1935.
Dancing the Charleston.
Mary Pickford.
'Granada' Tooting 1937.
Royal garden party 1926.
Prince of Wales, the film star image: by
courtesy of Central Press Photos Ltd.
Prince Edward at working men's club 1919.
Edward VIII with his Mother, Queen Mary.
Instrument of Abdication.
Duke and Duchess of Windsor 1937.
The Coronation 1937.
All the above pictures are by courtesy of
Radio Times Hulton Picture Library except
where otherwise acknowledged.